LIFE

to the

FULLEST

Books by Darrin Donnelly

THINK LIKE A WARRIOR
The Five Inner Beliefs That Make You Unstoppable

OLD SCHOOL GRIT
Times May Change, But the Rules for Success Never Do

RELENTLESS OPTIMISM
How a Commitment to Positive Thinking Changes Everything

LIFE TO THE FULLEST
A Story About Finding Your Purpose and Following Your Heart

LIFE
to the
FULLEST

A STORY ABOUT
FINDING YOUR PURPOSE
AND FOLLOWING YOUR HEART

Darrin Donnelly

Cover design by Damonza.

ISBN-13: 978-0692997215
ISBN-10: 0692997210

Visit us at: SportsForTheSoul.com

Sports for the Soul

Stories of Faith, Family, Courage, and Character.

This book is part of the *Sports for the Soul* series. For updates on this book, a sneak peek at future books, and a free newsletter that delivers advice and inspiration from top coaches, athletes, and sports psychologists, join us at: **SportsForTheSoul.com**.

The *Sports for the Soul* newsletter will help you:

- Find your calling and follow your passion
- Harness the power of positive thinking
- Build your self-confidence
- Attack every day with joy and enthusiasm
- Develop mental toughness
- Increase your energy and stay motivated
- Explore the spiritual side of success
- Be a positive leader for your family and your team
- Become the best version of yourself
- And much more…

Join us at: **SportsForTheSoul.com**.

Dedicated to my dad;

the man who taught me to always follow my heart.

And to Laura, Patrick, Katie, and Tommy;

who are everything to me.

Introduction

"If you love what you do, you'll never work a day in your life."

"Don't chase the money, follow your heart."

"Find your unique purpose; that's where you'll find happiness and success."

At some point in our lives, we've all heard variations of these phrases. They're often repeated by speakers at graduation ceremonies or motivational seminars.

Highly-successful people from all walks of life echo these words often. They inspire us to chase our biggest dreams. They encourage us to examine our souls and ask ourselves, "What was I truly *born* to do?" We're told that if we just find the answer to that question, everything else will fall into place and life will be a lot more fulfilling for us.

Steve Jobs, the founder of Apple, emphasized the importance of finding your purpose when, in a speech delivered to Stanford University's 2005 graduating class, he famously said, "The only way to do great work is to *love what you do*. If you haven't found it yet, keep looking. Don't settle. As with all matters of the heart, you'll know when you find it. … Have the courage to follow your heart and intuition. … Everything else is secondary."

Billionaire entrepreneur Richard Branson said, "Life's too short to waste your time doing things that don't light your fire. … *There is no greater thing you can do with your life and your work than follow your passions* — in a way that serves the world and you."

These entrepreneurial legends, Jobs and Branson, don't use any qualifiers. They make it sound as if your success *depends* on finding your true calling.

In the arts and entertainment industry, you'll find more of the same life guidance.

Stephen King, the most famous author of our time, said, "I never set a single word down on paper with the thought of being paid for it. … I have written because it fulfilled me. … *I did it for the pure joy of the thing.* And if you can do it for the joy, you can do it forever."

James Patterson, another hugely-popular author,

offered this succinct life wisdom: "To succeed, you have to work hard and *love what you do.*"

Ella Fitzgerald, the legendary singer, once said, *"Don't give up trying to do what you really want to do.* Where there is love and inspiration, I don't think you can go wrong."

Again and again, we hear the message to *follow your heart.* To chase *your* passion. To do what *you* love to do.

How about the sports world? The two most successful football coaches so far this century offer nearly identical advice.

Bill Belichick, the winner of more Super Bowls than any other coach in NFL history, says, "Don't pick a career for money or some other reason. *Do what you love,* because it will never feel like work."

Nick Saban, the most successful college football coach in modern history says the same thing: "It is imperative that we all make every effort to *do what we love.* My job is definitely a challenge, but I like what I do so much that it rarely seems like work to me."

Derek Jeter, one of the greatest baseball players ever, put it simply: "Dreams become realities when you love what you're doing."

Regardless of the career field, the most successful achievers agree: *you must follow your heart and live your unique purpose in order to be successful and happy.*

It's inspiring to hear advice like this. It forces us to reexamine our own lives and search for our purpose. It encourages each one of us to chase our dreams despite what any naysayers may try to tell us.

However, most of us also have a cynical voice in our head that hears such advice and counters with something like, "It's easy for *them* to say that. They've already made it big; they're hugely successful and wealthy. What if I chase my dream and fail?"

Or, that pessimistic voice says, "What if my dream job doesn't come with a million-dollar salary? I want to do what I love, but I've got bills to pay!"

And then there's this common rebuttal: "Sure, I'd love to follow my purpose, but I don't know *what* my purpose is!"

How do I find my purpose and is it safe to follow that purpose once I find it?

These are two of life's most important questions and these are the two questions this book will answer.

For years now, I've wanted to write a book that answered these questions, but I wanted to make sure I explored this topic from the perspective of someone whose life's purpose didn't make him or her a household name. After all, not all of us are called to be movie stars or CEOs of billion-dollar corporations.

When we're told to "dream big" and "live life to the fullest," it's easy to picture the jet-setting entrepreneurs, billionaire business icons, and world-famous athletes living a life of nonstop excitement and fame. And it's true, most of those people got to where they are by following their heart and doing what they love to do.

However, it's also true that following *your* heart and living *your* purpose may look a lot different. In fact, some of us would find that type of lifestyle quite unappealing.

One man's *biggest dream* might very well be to run a Fortune 500 company and buy a penthouse apartment in New York City. But another man's *biggest dream* might be a simpler lifestyle running a small family business in a close-knit community.

One man's idea of *life to the fullest* may mean trotting around the globe with one new adventure after another. But another man's idea of *life to the fullest* means a quieter life where weekly Sunday dinners with his family make him feel more fulfilled than anything else.

One man's dream may be to grace the cover of *Sports Illustrated* and coach a famous NFL team. Another man's dream life may be coaching a high school team in a small Midwestern town.

My point is not that one of the above examples is right and the other is wrong. It's simply that *your* purpose—following *your* heart—will be unique to you. Your biggest dream will not look like everyone else's and you can't let others dictate what your calling should be.

Despite what you may see on TV, purpose doesn't always correlate with fame. Living *life to the fullest* doesn't necessarily mean you'll end up on the cover of magazines and traveling the world nine months out of the year.

All around you, in everyday life, there are people who are living their purpose. They're the exception and not the norm, but you notice them when you see them. They're joyful at work, they take pride in what they do, they're driven to constantly learn and improve, and they seem so…*alive*, so…*happy*.

I'm thinking of the teachers who go above and beyond to make a difference in their students' lives, the family doctors who take a personal interest in the lives of their patients, the firefighters who believe it's their calling to save *other* people's lives, the soldiers who risk everything for their country, and the stay-at-home parents who lovingly and gladly sacrifice other personal desires to raise happy, successful, and respectful children.

These are people who have chosen to follow their heart and live their true purpose, even though they've never received fame and accolades for doing so.

I wanted to write a book about following your heart and living your purpose, but I wanted it to be applicable to *everyone* — not just those who are called to careers that can make them famous.

The main character in this book is John Callahan, a man in his mid-fifties who has spent his life following his heart. His life's dream was to follow in his father's footsteps as a high school football coach and he's lived that dream for the past three decades. But that dream is now being crushed. Just days before a state championship game, John receives news that his beloved school located in the heart of the "Rust Belt" is declaring bankruptcy and will be shutting down for good at the end of the year.

Everything John has worked his whole life for—his team, his community, his pension—is being taken away from him.

John finds himself angry at his long-deceased father for advising him to always follow his heart. He's angry at himself for being not taking "better" opportunities when they came along.

In a story that pays homage to the holiday classics, *It's a Wonderful Life* and *A Christmas Carol*, John receives a miraculous visit from his father on the eve of his team's final game. John is given the opportunity to revisit past moments in his life and he's offered the chance to see how his life would've turned out differently if he had chased more "practical" opportunities.

In the end, John sees the pros and cons of both life trajectories firsthand and must decide on the best path going forward.

This is a story about fathers and sons. It's a story about faith, family, and community. Most of all, it's a story about having the courage to follow your heart and live your true purpose.

As this story plays out, you will find the answers to two of life's most important questions:

How do I find my life's purpose?

Is it safe to follow that purpose?

Darrin Donnelly
SportsForTheSoul.com

"Never let the odds keep you from pursuing what you know in your heart you were meant to do."

- SATCHEL PAIGE

1

All my life, I only wanted to be one thing: the head football coach at St. Mary's High School in Kingstown, Ohio. That's it. That was my big dream.

That sounds strange to a lot of people. They wonder, *Why would anyone want to stay in the same small town they grew up in and coach at the same high school they attended? Don't you want to dream bigger? Don't you want to get out of that "dying" town and see what else is out there?*

Like everyone else, there have been many times where I've wondered what my life would've been like if I had done things differently. I've had opportunities to coach in college, even got offered an entry-level job in the NFL once. Though I haven't received any job offers in recent years, I'm pretty confident I would've done well in those next-level jobs if I had taken them. Coaching is coaching—no matter what level you're at—and I've won nearly ninety percent of my games as head coach here at St. Mary's High. I think I could've been successful at the college and pro levels — *if* that's what I had wanted to do with my life.

And sure, I look at my little brother, Andy, and I see a guy who has made millions of dollars working for an investment bank on Wall Street and then starting his own financial firm. He's got a luxury apartment in Manhattan, a beach house in the Hamptons, and a mansion in Palm Beach, Florida. I'd be lying if I told you there weren't times I was jealous of his financial freedom and all the things he's been able to provide for his daughter, like the Harvard education he was able to afford for her.

Years ago, I was visiting Andy at his mansion in Florida (this was back when we were still talking to each other, but more on that later). I had asked to borrow some money for a financial crunch I'd been in and my brother obliged, but not before telling me, as we stood on his expansive balcony that looked out onto the Atlantic Ocean, "John, I hope this situation serves as a lesson for you. You're capable of so much more than being a *high school* coach. And don't give me that line Dad used to give us about following your heart. If I had followed my heart, I'd be a broke guitar player spending my nights in dive bars. Work is called *work* for a reason; it's not supposed to be fun. I don't like my job. I'm not ashamed to admit that. But I'd rather make millions doing a job I hate than worry about paying the bills every month. I'd rather do exactly what I'm doing if it means I won't have to ask friends and family for handouts. Look around you; the payoff for what I do is obviously worth it. You should think about that."

It was painful to keep my mouth shut during this condescending little lesson he gave me, but I didn't argue with him. Judging from his Facebook posts, he's always either closing another million-dollar deal or setting off on another lavish vacation. Clearly, my little brother enjoys the fruits of his labor.

But those "better" jobs I was offered weren't my calling. I never fantasized about coaching in the Super Bowl or becoming the next Gordon Gekko. For as long as I can remember I dreamed of being one thing: the head coach of the St. Mary's High School Panthers, just like my dad, Big Jim Callahan, had been.

And for twenty-eight years, I had been living that dream. That is, until it came crashing down just two days before the biggest game of my coaching career.

2

It was Thursday, December 1, 2016 — exactly one week after Thanksgiving and five days after we defeated Rockwell High School, 29-28, in the Division VII state semifinals of the Ohio high school football playoffs.

Up until about eight o'clock that evening, it had been a near-perfect late-fall day here in the Midwest.

Temperatures were in the forties and a cool, misty rain had settled over Kingstown for much of the day. Weather that was made for football.

We had just finished our last full-contact practice of the season and the boys were in good spirits. As were us coaches. The preparation work was mostly done. We were ready for Saturday's state championship game.

Saturday would mark the conclusion of my twenty-eighth season as head coach of the Panthers. It would be my seventh state championship game, which would tie me for the fourth-most state championship appearances by a head coach in the history of Ohio high school football.

There was one state record that I held all to myself, though it's not one to be proud of. I had lost all six of my previous state championship games, which gave me the unfortunate distinction of being the only coach in Ohio high school football history to *lose* so many title games.

Like I said, it's not a record I'm proud of.

But this year was going to be different. It would be lucky number seven. I could sense there was something special about this team. No one had expected us to make it as far as we had. After a 1-2 start, we pulled off one improbable win after another. We were now 13-2 and headed to state with momentum on our side.

Dare I say, we were a team of *destiny*.

After practice, I stopped by the candle-lit grotto located at the entrance to our parish campus—a campus that consisted of St. Mary's Catholic Church, St. Mary's Elementary School, St. Mary's High School, a gym that also served as the parish community center, and a football stadium named after my father: Jim Callahan Stadium. I knelt down on one of the grotto's kneelers and said a quick prayer. I did this every day before heading home.

I then crunched my way through fallen leaves as I walked the two blocks down Oak Street from the St. Mary's campus to the old two-story brick home I lived in.

I could smell fireplaces burning in the cold night air. I know a lot of people hate the cold winters here in the Midwest, but I wasn't one of them. I loved the crisp air in the fall and winter. I found it exhilarating. I loved the smell of leaves on the ground, of snow on the way, and of that burning firewood wafting out of chimneys.

The sun had already set and in the distance I could hear the comforting sound of a train's horn blowing as it rumbled down the tracks.

As I made my way home, I inhaled deeply and smiled. *Life is good*, I thought to myself. *Life is good*.

My home was four doors down from the house I had grown up in—the house Mom still lived in, along with one of my sisters, Sherry, and her husband, Mike, who were both sacrificing personal space and freedom to help take care of Mom.

Two blocks further down lived another sister of mine, Patti, and her husband, Alonzo Carter.

Alonzo and I had been close friends ever high school, when we shared the backfield on that famous 1981 team—the team that *USA Today* named National Champions. I was the quarterback and he was one of the halfbacks in our Wishbone offense. Despite the fact that we ran a three-back offense, Alonzo rushed for more than 1,700 yards that season. He played his college ball at Ohio State and spent four seasons in the NFL. As the quarterback for that National Championship team, I would always be best known as the guy who got the ball to "A.C."

Alonzo was now the principal at St. Mary's High School, which made him my boss—though he liked to jokingly say that he wasn't sure who was who's boss in this football-crazed community.

I walked out from the cold and into our home to be greeted by a roaring fireplace. Life was indeed good.

My son, Micky, was shoveling down a bowl of Gina's famous chili—famous to us, at least. Micky was our youngest of four, a junior linebacker at St. Mary's. Our other three children had moved out; my two daughters, Lisa and Angie, were in college and my oldest son, Jimmy, was a teacher at St. Mary's

…cks coach on my staff.

…re high school sweethearts who got

…er college. We would be celebrating

…d wedding anniversary in June. It

takes a special kind of person to be a coach's wife. A coach's spouse lives through every victory and defeat right along with the coach. Gina has always been my strongest supporter, my voice of reason, and the best wife a guy could ever ask for. She's always there to lift me up when I'm doubting myself and she's there to remind me what's most important in life when I lose touch with my priorities of faith, family, and *then* football—in that order! She's also there to kick me in the butt whenever I need to be motivated. I love her more every day.

Our life revolves around the football season. Coaching is an all-consuming profession and from August to December every year, I'm not the most attentive husband and father. But no matter what, no matter how crazy things get, we *always* have dinner together. That was the promise I made to her when I first took this job. The only time my dad, Big Jim, ever missed a dinner with my mom and us kids was if he was traveling to a game. I made sure I did the same with my wife and kids.

On Sundays, that family dinner was a cookout that involved many of my extended family members who still lived in Kingstown. We'd usually grill steaks, burgers, or bratwursts—even in freezing temperatures.

No matter what is going on, that Sunday dinner brings our entire family back together each and every week. It's always my mom, my kids, my siblings, and those nieces and nephews who are still in town. Those of us siblings who lived in Kingstown would take turns hosting. Sometimes, these Sunday dinners included my two uncles and three aunts who also lived in Kingstown. A few of my cousins have also been known to stop by every now and then.

I realize all this sounds either very sentimental or very lame—depending on your viewpoint. Living so close to the people and places you've known pretty much your entire life can sound like an idealistic dream or a stifling nightmare. I suppose it depends on who those people are and what those places mean to you.

I don't want to romanticize my life to the point of acting like I don't have a care in the world. Coaching is a stressful profession and despite winning nearly ninety percent of my games, I've experienced a few off-seasons where my job was in jeopardy—I was a coach on "the hot seat," as it's known throughout the sports world. Those made for miserable times as I wondered what I would do if I was fired from the school I loved so dearly.

Like most people, Gina and I have had our fair share of hard times trying to make ends meet. We've struggled right along with the other citizens of Kingstown as our community lost good-paying jobs, longtime friends moved away, and too much crime moved in. There are times when the pressure of my job has gotten to me and I've felt overworked and overstressed. I've sometimes struggled with guilt about the long hours I've put into the football team when I should've been putting in more time at home. We've had family spats and falling-outs with friends over issues that seem silly in hindsight.

In other words, we've faced most the same issues everybody faces.

Despite that, the good times have far outweighed the bad. I've never felt alone in this community. I've always had people I can count on. It's quiet here. It's friendly here. I've always found peace of mind here. This place is my home.

I've always felt that living here and coaching at St. Mary's High was my calling, my life's purpose. It's rarely been easy, but it's always been fulfilling.

I've always been...*happy* here.

But that all changed when Alonzo knocked on my door that Thursday evening.

3

For the few weeks prior to the knock on my door, I knew something wasn't right with Alonzo. Normally a life-of-the-party type of guy, he had been quiet and distant at our Sunday cookouts. When I saw him at school, he looked stressed and in a hurry. I didn't see him stopping to chat with students and faculty as he usually did. He was mostly in his office, the door closed.

This uncommon behavior struck me as peculiar, but I was so consumed with our playoff run that I hadn't spent much time worrying about it. We all get into funks from time to time; even the jovial Alonzo Carter is entitled to one here and there.

But as soon as I answered the door and saw Alonzo on my front porch Thursday night, I knew something serious had happened.

It was normal for Alonzo to stop by unannounced since we lived so close to each other. But usually he'd greet me on the porch with a big smile, asking me if I wanted to hit Patti's Place, the bar and restaurant down on Main Street that my sister (his wife) owned, to watch a game and have a drink or two. Other times, he'd show up on my front porch to challenge me to an impromptu game of basketball or racquetball. Sometimes, he'd ask me to come down to the school with him to help with an urgent issue.

Regardless of the reason, he always greeted me with a cheerful smile that forced me to comply with whatever request he had. Alonzo was the type of guy you never wanted to let down. Mostly because he would never let *you* down, but also because he was always such a positive person to be around.

On this night, Alonzo wasn't smiling. He had a stern, worried look on his face as he stood on my porch with his hands tucked tight into his coat pockets.

"Hey John, you got a second?" he asked quietly.

"Of course, come on in," I said.

"Actually, you mind talking to me out here?"

Another clear sign something was wrong.

"Sure," I said, stepping onto the front porch and closing the door behind me. "What's going on? You don't look well."

"I'm not," he said. "And I don't want Gina or

Micky to hear what I'm about to tell you. They'll find out soon enough."

"You're scaring me, buddy, what's going on?"

He sat down on the porch ledge, his eyes fixed downward.

"I don't know how to say this," he said. "But I want you to hear from me before you see it in the paper tomorrow morning."

"Is Patti okay? Are your kids okay?" I was panicking now and my mind started cooking up disastrous scenarios.

"They're fine," Alonzo said. "For now."

"Spit it out, A.C. What is this about?"

"St. Mary's." He motioned his head down the street toward the school. From my front porch you could see the church steeple in the center of our campus glowing in the night sky. Then he looked up at me. "The high school. It's done. They're closing us down."

"What do you mean?" I asked. "Who's *they* and what are they doing?"

"The archdiocese. They're shutting us down. We have to declare bankruptcy. It's finally happening. St. Mary's High School is closing down."

I felt blood rush to my head and I plopped down in a chair across from Alonzo. I rubbed my forehead, which felt hot despite the cold night air.

"We've heard this before," I said.

Most parochial schools are constantly struggling to keep their doors open and St. Mary's High School was no exception. Every year, we'd hear rumors about budget shortfalls and whispers about being shut down, but they were just rumors. We always found a way to stay open.

Alonzo shook his head.

"Not like this," he said. "This is the real deal."

He had openly discussed his worries about budget issues before, but never with such dire certainty.

"How short are we?" I asked. "How much do we need to raise?"

"We're more than broke," he said. "We're deep in the hole and the archdiocese can't make up the difference anymore. We're not talking car washes and pledge drives to get out of this one. Everything is gone. And I mean it when I say, *everything*."

He looked me in the eye when he said *everything*.

"What does that mean, everything?" I asked.

"It means…it means our pensions are gone too."

"That's impossible," I said. "They can't do that. There are laws to protect our pensions."

"Tell that to my dad and all those guys who spent their life working at Kingstown Steel and Pipe." Alonzo said, referencing this town's largest employer up until 1985. "Bankruptcy is bankruptcy. There's nowhere to get the money. We've tried everything we can think of. Every teacher will be let go with less than one year's severance and that's it. It's gone and it ain't coming back. It's a tragedy. *Another* tragedy to hit this town."

"This is crazy," I said. "I'm fifty-three years old; I can't just start over. What am I supposed to do? Teach until I'm eighty-three to build my retirement back up?"

"I don't know, John, I don't know. What I do know is that I'm in the same boat. We all are."

"There must be some way," I said. "There's *got* to be. It's just like we tell the kids, there's a solution to every problem. We just have to find it. We just have to find a way. How much money do we need?"

"The decision is made; it came down from the top," Alonzo said. "There's nothing we can do.

Believe me, I've tried everything. We're not talking about keeping the lights on for another year. We'd need to replenish everything. We'd need enough money to convince the archdiocese that we could be self-sustaining for years to come. I've spent the last six months trying to hold them off, trying to find another way. There isn't one."

"I know there's a number," I said. "And I know you know it. Shoot me straight. What would it take? How much money do we need to stay open?"

Alonzo shook his head. "You don't want to hear it."

"Yes, I do. What's it gonna' take?" I stood up now, charged with adrenaline. We *were* going to find a way. We *had* to.

"Nine-point-eight million."

I sat back down. Deflated.

4

Alonzo might as well have said we needed $9.8 *billion*. Every spring and summer, we had to beg and plead our way to raising our goal of $100,000 from the parish, our alumni, and anyone else in the community. We used all types of fundraisers, auctions, and pledge drives to try to reach that goal. Our enrollment had been shrinking over the years and of those students that did attend, only about half could afford to pay the full tuition. This meant that the tuition to attend St. Mary's High School ended up covering far less than half of the school's operating cost for each student. Parish funds helped cover some of the difference and the archdiocese covered the majority of it. The archdiocese's portion had grown more each year as we ran up more and more debt to keep our doors open.

The annual $100,000 fundraising goal was a rather arbitrary figure. It never made a serious dent in the school's financial stability; it was just enough to ease the bleeding budget and convince the archdiocese that we were doing our part. Sometimes we hit that number, most times we didn't.

Now, we would need to raise *ninety-eight* times that amount if we had any chance of keeping St. Mary's High School open. Alonzo explained that the archdiocese had ruled that unless we could raise enough money to wipe out our debt and set us on the path toward operating primarily off of the interest earned annually, they had no choice but to shut us down. The archdiocese was financially strained itself and could no longer cover our increasing expenses and debt.

I always considered myself an optimist, but even I wasn't naïve enough to believe that kind of money was a possibility.

Kingstown had fallen on hard times over the last four decades and the people who lived here weren't stingy with their money; they were simply tapped out.

Alonzo told me that the news of our school's closure would be made public Friday morning in the *Kingstown Daily Herald*. He said he tried to convince the paper to hold off on publishing the story, at least until after Saturday's game.

"They said it's too important of a story," Alonzo said. "I'm sorry, John. I know it's going to be a huge distraction for the team."

We talked for a good twenty minutes before Alonzo had me convinced this was really happening. Every option I suggested had already been thought of and tried. When Alonzo left, I couldn't bring myself to tell Gina and Micky the news.

"What were you two doing out in the cold so long?" Gina asked.

"Getting some fresh air," I said. "In fact, I'm going out for a walk."

"Is everything okay?" she asked.

"Just need to clear my head." I grabbed my coat, kissed Gina, and walked back outside. She knew something was wrong.

I had an urge to head towards the school, maybe stop at the grotto or the church to pray for a miracle.

But what good would that do? I thought to myself.

Moments like this challenge a man's faith. I was boiling inside and my head was racing with worst-case scenarios.

What would we do now? I'd have to find a new job and we'd surely have to move. Where would we go? How long would I have to work to rebuild my retirement?

And what about Saturday's game? How could I possibly focus on the game with all this going on?

How do I tell Gina? How do I tell Micky?

Everything I've given my life to, it's all…gone. In a matter of months, life as I've known it will be gone forever.

My home – in every sense of the word – will be taken from me.

I walked with an angry, purposeful stride. I took a right turn toward Main Street, two blocks away.

I walked this path often. There was something peaceful about the lamplights along Main Street at night, even more so now with Christmas lights outlining the roofs of all the shops and restaurants — even the abandoned places with boarded-up windows got the Christmas-light treatment.

Things had been a lot worse in this town. The closed-up shops used to outnumber the open ones two-to-one. These days, that ratio had been reversed, but the vacancies were still a constant reminder of where our town had been and where it was now.

Kingstown is the type of place that has come to epitomize what is known as the "Rust Belt" of America. It had once reached a population of more than 55,000. Hard-working people made good money here. You could work for Kingstown Steel and Pipe, one of the two large textile plants, or any of the other mid-sized factories, and make enough to support a family and send your kids to college. Everyone had union jobs and this place was known for its strong work ethic, its fair wages, and its can-do attitude.

Then, the outsourcing began.

Layoffs started accelerating in the 1970s. Only "short-term" layoffs, the workers were told, "Just until the economy improves." But once they left, the jobs never came back. One textile plant shut down in 1977, another in 1979. The town could survive without the textile factories, but when Kingstown Steel and Pipe stopped laying off workers and decided to shut its doors for good in 1985, that was the deathblow.

It was a story that played out across the Industrial Midwest. Our situation wasn't unique and I suppose it could've been worse. Places like Youngstown, Ohio; Flint, Michigan; and Aliquippa, Pennsylvania; had it much worse than us.

The sudden loss of jobs and the economic decline

here in Kingstown ripped apart families. Those that could find new jobs found them in new faraway towns.

Those that couldn't find jobs held onto that glimmer of hope that things would somehow someway turn around for this community. There were always rumors about a new company coming in to reopen one of the shuttered factories. Sometimes it would happen, but the jobs were temporary, the pay was low, and the capacity was minimal compared to what it had been before.

With a decrease in jobs and wages came an increase in crime. In the late 1980s and early 1990s, things were particularly bad. Drugs became all-too-common in this shrinking town. Robberies went up. Our house was burglarized twice. It wasn't considered safe to walk down Main Street after dark.

Those were the desperate times.

Slowly, the people clinging to hope realized the jobs their parents and grandparents had were gone and they were *never* coming back to Kingstown.

The population of Kingstown fell to less than 30,000, which is where it stands today. In the early 2000s, the town quit begging for new jobs to bring us back to where we were and instead accepted the fact that we would have to reinvent ourselves. We would never again be a thriving factory town, but maybe we could turn ourselves into a charming Midwestern small town.

That was the plan we came up with as a community.

Abandoned homes were torn down and ugly abandoned lots were turned into parks.

The Kingstown Steel and Pipe factory was finally torn down in 2006. People hated to do it because despite the rusted-out exterior, the ugly acres of garbage, the grimy smokestacks, and the broken-glass windows, there was always that glimmer of hope that one day the factory would be reopened. That huge, imposing property nestled along the picturesque river represented this town for decades. As the factory goes, so goes the town—people had always been told. When the city imploded the Kingstown Steel and Pipe factory that had stood for generations, I saw men of all ages wiping away tears.

The love-hate relationship with that factory was finally over.

For three decades, the people of Kingstown

engineered several campaigns to revitalize the downtown, to rid the city of crime, to build new parks and community centers. Some of these ambitious campaigns were more successful than others, but all-in-all, things *had* improved since those darkest days of despair.

The three public high schools that were once here had been consolidated into the one that remains today.

The downtown may not have been as busy as it was back when I was a kid, but it was safe to walk down Main Street after dark again. The people who had stayed here, for the most part, had found new jobs. Kingstown had come to terms with what it would be — no longer a small city, now a small town.

Our town *had* gotten better. It *had* been cleaned up. We had weathered the storm and survived. Did we still have a ways to go? Sure. Did kids leave town and never come back once they graduated high school? For the most part, yes.

But things were better than they had been. We had turned a corner. That's what I had been telling myself for the past thirty years. I had to believe it.

Through all the ups and downs, the St. Mary's

school and parish had survived. Once a Division II program (the second-largest classification in the state of Ohio), St. Mary's High School was now a Division VII program (the smallest classification in Ohio). We went from more than two hundred students per class in the 1980s to less than two hundred students in the whole high school today. And while the pews weren't as crowded as they once were every Sunday morning, our big, beautiful church still stood tall—literally and figuratively.

You could always see that tall church steeple from downtown. It stood for something. It was a symbol of resilience. It said that no matter what kind of adversity Kingstown went through, *this* sacred place was safe. *This* place was protected. No matter how hard things got, God would protect St. Mary's. It was *safe* to trust.

At least—it had stood for those things up until Alonzo gave me the devastating news that Thursday night. Either God couldn't or wouldn't protect this place any longer. St. Mary's High would be the latest institution to fall in Kingstown. It would force me and my family to leave the place we loved, the place that had been our home our entire lives.

As I walked the sidewalk along Main Street, an elderly man named Frank—a guy who had played for Big Jim back in the 1950s, stopped and said, "Good luck on Saturday, Coach."

It took a lot of willpower for me to stop. I wanted to keep walking with my head down as I stewed. But, I forced myself to stop and acknowledge Frank. I thanked him and told him I liked our chances. I asked him how his family was, if he was ready for Christmas, and if he'd be at the game on Saturday. Small talk that might seem meaningless to some, but I knew it mattered. People need to stop and acknowledge each other. People need to let each other know they care about one another. That's what Big Jim always taught me. And even though my mind was racing with fear, worry, and anger; those lessons were imbedded in me.

At the corner of 5th Street and Main stood Bob's Diner, a 24-hour greasy-spoon restaurant I'd been eating at since I was a kid. It had opened in 1951 and still served the best burgers in town—contrary to how hard my sister Patti tried to claim the burgers at her restaurant were better.

As I approached, I saw Charlie Kowalski putting

something on the front window.

Charlie was the third-generation owner of the diner his grandfather had started. Charlie was also the middle linebacker for St. Mary's in 1989, my first season as head coach of the Panthers.

"Somebody break a window, Charlie?" I asked.

He looked at me and forced a smile. "Nah, Coach. Having to do something I was hoping I'd never have to do. I've put it off for far too long."

When I reached the window, I saw that Charlie wasn't doing patchwork or placing a menu out front. He was putting a hand-made sign on the front window. It read: FOR SALE.

"Oh, Charlie," I said. "I'm so sorry. It can't be."

"It is what it is." He shrugged. "I've been putting this off for years. It's finally time. It is what it is."

Who was I kidding? This place hasn't turned the corner and it never will. This town is dying a slow death and it will never be revived.

I've wasted my life trying to convince myself otherwise.

5

When I got home and told Gina about the school closing, she refused to believe it. She wasn't hysterical or panicked; she simply refused to believe it.

"It won't happen," she said matter-of-factly. She even managed a smile. "You'll see. We'll find a way to save it. We always do."

"Not this time, this is the real deal," I said, repeating the same phrase Alonzo had used on me.

"We've heard it before," she said. "We'll find a way."

"I don't think you understand what is happening. The sooner we both accept the facts, the easier this will be."

"I'm not sure I appreciate your condescending tone." She wasn't snapping at me, simply stating a fact. "You worry too much, John, you always have."

Gina's sunny outlook only made me angrier.

"You don't realize how serious this is," I said. "This is really happening. Our life is falling apart."

"What's that sign in your office say?" Gina asked. *"Things have a way of working themselves out if we just remain positive."*

She was repeating a quote that hung on my office wall. It was a quote from Lou Holtz, the former Notre Dame football coach.

"Yeah, well, not this time," I said with a bitter tone that surprised even me.

That night, I tossed and turned and slept an hour or two tops. In the morning, the *Kingstown Daily Herald* headline made the news official with its front-page headline: ST. MARY'S TO CLOSE.

Two sub-headlines followed:

"High school will shut down at end of the school year."

"Legendary football program will play its final game Saturday."

Gina didn't say it, but the look on her face told me that the screaming headlines put a dent in her optimistic outlook. She was worried, just like me.

"What does this mean?" Micky asked at the breakfast table. "I'm going to be a senior next year, am I supposed to just find a new school? Are we going to have to move? My friends are all here.

Meghan is here." Meghan was his girlfriend, also a junior at St. Mary's.

"We'll figure something out," I said.

"This isn't fair," he said, pain in his eyes. "They can't do this right before my senior year."

"Life's not always fair," I said.

"Oh, that's *real* helpful," he said with a glare.

"Let's not get carried away," Gina said. "None of this is final."

"It looks pretty final to me," Micky said, pointing at the headline.

"Me too," I said. That earned me a glare from Gina as well.

6

I expected there to be a larger-than-normal crowd at Darla's Donut Shop Friday morning and sure enough, a couple dozen people were waiting out front on the corner of 2nd and Elm.

Most mornings, I took a one block detour on my way to school and stopped in at Darla's for coffee and an occasional donut. Located right next door to Dave's Barbershop (yes, Darla and Dave were husband and wife), there was usually a handful of people waiting here each fall morning and they were armed with questions and opinions about our football team. My dad, Big Jim, had made stopping here part of his morning ritual when he was head coach and I had continued the tradition when I got the job.

"The best way to handle critics is to face them head-on," Big Jim had told me. "You'd be surprised how opinions change when someone has to say it to your face."

Today, everyone wanted answers about the

school.

"Is it true?" was the first question shouted at me.

"Unfortunately, yes." I said.

"How long have you known about this?" someone yelled with an accusatory tone, as though I might've been hiding this secret.

"I found out last night."

"How could you not see this coming?" an angry voice shouted from the back of the pack. "My son's a freshman and I've got two more in the grade school. What are we supposed to do?"

I shook my head. "I wish I knew." Some questions couldn't be answered.

"What do you need from us to save the school?" This question came from Mike Murphy. He was the third-generation owner of Victory Sportswear, a clothing company based right here in Kingstown. One of the few manufacturing jobs that remained, they employed more than one thousand people.

I paused, unsure how to answer that question. The crowd waited. The *Daily Herald* had quoted Alonzo's $9.8 million figure. They all knew the answer. They wanted me to tell them something different.

"That's really kind of you, Mike—of all of you," I said. "But I don't think there's anything we can do. The figure in the paper is correct. It's...it's over, folks. We're done."

I could've sworn I heard a few gasps. Saying those words out loud made it even more official—to the crowd and to me.

"How are you going to keep the boys focused for Saturday?" another person asked.

"I wish I knew," I said.

Again, some questions couldn't be answered.

7

Friday was a blur. I taught Religion class at St. Mary's High School and no matter what lessons had been planned for this day, the conversation shifted to fears about what would happen to everyone next year and how God could let this happen to our school. It was like an all-day counseling session.

Discussing the problem of evil—why a good God would allow bad things to happen—was common in my class, but the issue was suddenly more than a hypothetical question about the pain and suffering in the world "out there." The kids now wanted real answers about why God was allowing *their* lives to suddenly be turned upside down here and now. They wanted to know why God was abandoning them. I wanted answers too.

In my thirty years of teaching this class, I'd never found a truly satisfying answer to the question.

Sure, I could quote St. Augustine and St. Thomas Aquinas, who both concluded that God would only permit an evil if a greater good could eventually be brought out of it. And I could point my students to the Book of Job, which ultimately tells us that we can't begin to see all that God sees—we don't see how everything will play out the way God does, so we simply have to trust that He knows what He's doing; surely his track record has earned him the benefit of the doubt.

But these were theological answers. They were thought-provoking responses that gave *some* peace to the most difficult question of faith. But when the question is suddenly about *you* and *your* life in the moment, there is no sufficient answer. Throughout the day, the only answer that seemed to bring the students' comfort was the reminder: "You're not alone in this; we're all in it together."

Friday's practice after school had a similar tone. It was the final walkthrough before Saturday's state championship game—a game that would likely be the biggest one these kids *ever* played in. It should have been one of the most exciting, energetic times of these young men's lives. It should have been a focused practice of last-minute preparations. But the players weren't thinking much about football; they were thinking about what would happen next year.

In the truest sense of the word, Saturday would be the last time any of these boys would play together as St. Mary's Panthers.

There would be no *next year* for the underclassmen. For the seniors — as if playing for a state championship wasn't high enough stakes — they now had the *added* pressure of representing St. Mary's High School in the final game this proud football program would *ever* play.

I did my best to conduct a "business as usual" practice. I told them all I believed in them, that we were well prepared, and that I knew they would make St. Mary's proud tomorrow afternoon.

But just like the players, I couldn't stop thinking about everything else that was going on.

8

I had been the head coach at St. Mary's High School for twenty-eight seasons. During that span, I'd won 89.7% of my games, which made me one of the winningest head coaches in the history of Ohio. But never once had I ended the season with a victory.

During the previous twenty-seven seasons, my teams made the playoffs twenty-four times. Six of those times we made it all the way to the state championship. But not once did we win it all.

Even during the three rare seasons where we failed (just barely) to qualify for the playoffs, I *still* lost my final game of the regular season.

How does that happen? You would think the law of averages would play out. You would think that a coach who wins nearly ninety percent of his games would find a way to win at least *one* of his final games.

Just once I'd like to know what it's like to walk off the field for the final time in a season with a victory. Just once I'd like to know what an offseason feels like where I'm not stewing and replaying in my head every single decision of that final loss. Just once I want to know how my dad, Big Jim, felt *eleven* different times when he walked off the field with a season-ending victory and a state championship.

Why could I win so many games, but never the BIG game?

Certainly, our fans wanted an answer to this question as well. After all, my dad had no trouble winning the big game when he was here.

Big Jim Callahan was named head coach at St. Mary's High in 1956, when he was just twenty-six years old. He had played his college ball at Notre Dame for Frank Leahy and he brought the lessons he learned from one of college football's greatest coaches ever to St. Mary's.

My dad coached for thirty-three seasons at St. Mary's. Actually, thirty-two-and-a-half seasons. Six games into the 1988 season, Big Jim collapsed on the practice field and died of a brain aneurysm. It was a fluke thing, something you couldn't see coming. One minute he was coaching his quarterbacks, the next his lifeless body had dropped to the ground.

I was an assistant coach on his staff for the 1987

and 1988 seasons. When he died, his longtime defensive coordinator was named head coach. With heavy hearts, we lost in the first round of the playoffs that year and St. Mary's hired me to take over as head coach in 1989.

From 1956-1987, Big Jim made St. Mary's High School not only the most successful team in Ohio, but he made the team a *national* football power. He won eleven state championships and three national championships: 1972, 1978, and 1981.

Following in a legend's footsteps is never easy. No matter what you do, you're going to be compared to your predecessor. And it's only natural that the legend becomes more beloved with each passing year. The shadow he casts over you gets bigger and bigger.

I'm not sure if it's easier or harder to follow a legend if that legend is your father. All I can say is that I never felt like I couldn't do it. I never believed that I wouldn't be able to continue the tradition Big Jim had established. I never doubted that I too would be racking up state titles just like my old man did for thirty-plus seasons.

I never wanted to be anything other than the head

coach at St. Mary's High School. I wanted to be just like my father, my hero, Big Jim Callahan.

During my first four years as head coach, we never lost a regular season game. We made it to the state championship during my first season in 1989, then again in 1991. I lost those state title games and I heard the offseason grumblings about whether I had what it took to win the big one, but I believed it was only a matter of time before I'd prove my doubters wrong. After all, in just four seasons I'd made it to the big game twice — something few teams *ever* get to do. Now, I just had to find a way to *win* that big game.

Every time the pressure turned up on me and my seat got hotter after a playoff loss, we'd go on a run the next year that took us to state. We made it to the state championship again in 1996 and 1999. In 2005, I had the most talented player to ever play for St. Mary's High (more on him later). We again made it to state and we again lost.

Even though we didn't win the state championship, the school board couldn't justify firing a coach who had just led his team to the state finals. (Though, I've heard that those school board votes on whether to keep me or fire me were razor-thin at times.)

In 2012, I had the most talented overall team I've ever coached. We were outstanding on both sides of the ball. You could make the argument that there had never been a more talented team from a school this small in the history of Ohio. *Eight* players from that senior class went on to play Division 1 college football. We rolled through an undefeated regular season and beat all our playoff opponents by at least three touchdowns. This was supposed to be our year — with so much talent, even *I* wouldn't be able to screw it up. We were the heavy favorites to win the Division VI state championship that year. But, everything that could go wrong did go wrong that afternoon. We had five turnovers and lost on a last-second field goal.

Six state final appearances, six losses. And we had a second-half lead in every single one of those state championship games.

I wasn't the only guy in Kingstown who thought I might be cursed.

It also wasn't lost on anyone that St. Mary's had not won a state title since Kingstown Steel and Pipe shut its doors in the spring of 1985. Big Jim's final state championship was 1984. A public high school from Kingstown hadn't won a title since then either.

Maybe I wasn't the only one cursed. Maybe the whole town was cursed—destined to never again rise to the top...of anything.

9

My focus on Friday night should have been on one thing and one thing only: Saturday's state championship game. This would be the final game in our school's history — a fact that still didn't seem real to me — and I owed it to this team and every other team this school has ever fielded to give this one everything I've got. This would be the game St. Mary's High would be forever remembered for.

Yet, my focus wasn't on the game.

All I could think about was whether or not I should give *The Senior Speech* after Saturday's game.

The Senior Speech was a tradition at St. Mary's. It was started by Big Jim and I had carried it on. The underclassmen heard whispers about it from the time they were freshmen, some of them even before. The speech was confidential. It was for the seniors only.

Win or lose, after the final game of the season, when all the standard postgame activities were finished, the underclassmen would be asked to leave the locker room. Once the underclassmen had left, the room was closed off and the seniors took a seat.

The Senior Speech wasn't particularly long and I suppose that was by design. Just as Big Jim promised it would be, it was the most memorable speech any St. Mary's player would ever hear.

Big Jim had a booming voice that matched his larger-than-life persona. He had a tall and broad body built for being the defensive tackle he was at Notre Dame, and when he gave *The Senior Speech*, his voice thundered through the room. He spoke in short-sentence spurts, sort of like barking out a pre-snap cadence.

Here's how Big Jim gave *The Senior Speech* to me after my final game in 1981 — and it's how I've tried to give it every year of my head coaching career…

"Men, the reason I wait to give this speech until after the final game of the season is because I know you'll remember it for the rest of your lives. This is the last time you'll ever sit in the locker room as a St. Mary's Panther and what I'm about to tell you will stay with you forever.

"As you walk out that door tonight and begin the rest of your life, I want you to take with you what

I'm about to tell you. This is the most important life advice I can give you."

Big Jim let his words sink in for a moment and then turned to the chalk board behind him (I used a whiteboard these days). He wrote down three words: *FOLLOW YOUR HEART!*

"What you decide to do with the rest of your life is completely up to you. And for most people, this is the most important *and* the most difficult decision they'll ever make.

"But I'm here to tell you it doesn't have to be a difficult decision. In fact, it shouldn't be.

"Finding your purpose in life is not made in one single moment, but in a series of important moments. Where will you go to college? What will you major in? Who will you marry? Where will you live? What kind of profession will you enter?

"These are important questions that will determine the quality of your life. Lots of people agonize over these questions for decades and never find adequate answers. Adding to the complexity is the fact that the answers to these questions can and will change throughout your life. Your life's purpose at age twenty-five might look a lot different when you're fifty-five.

"But I'm going to give you the secret to making sure you find the answers you need whenever you're faced with these important life decisions.

"The secret is written on that board behind me: *Follow Your Heart!*"

Big Jim turned around and tapped the chalk board with his coarse knuckle.

"Follow your heart," he repeated. "If you do that, you'll never go wrong.

"Whenever you're faced with an important life decision, simply ask yourself, 'Am I following my heart?'

"Don't worry about what the world says you should do and don't worry about what all the naysayers might say about your dreams. Only *you* know what God put in your heart and you have to follow that vision.

"Now, this isn't always going to be easy to do. As I mentioned, there are complexities involved.

"There are five components to life that must all interact with each other for you to be happy and successful. Sometimes, it can feel like these five components are conflicting with each other.

"How do you handle these conflicts? By getting your priorities straight. Not all five components are equal; you have to prioritize each one."

Big Jim turned around and wrote on the chalk board: *NO. 1 – FAITH*.

"The first and most important component of living your life's purpose is your faith.

"Men, wherever you are and whatever you're doing, if you find yourself wondering what you should do next; you need to ask yourself, 'What does God want me to do?' And then, listen to your heart. God will speak to you. You know what's right and what's wrong and you'll know the Holy Spirit when you feel it.

"Listen to God. In all things and in all ways, put God first. Every other decision will get a lot easier after that."

Big Jim then wrote on the chalkboard: *NO. 2 – FAMILY*.

"The next most important component of your life is your family. Right now, that means honoring your mom and dad, supporting your siblings, being there for your friends, your teammates, and your classmates—people who are like family to you.

"But soon, you'll be starting a family of your own. If putting God first is the most important decision of your life, who you decide to marry is the second-most important. Marry right and everything else falls into place.

"Honor your wife and always treat her with the upmost respect. You'll have problems, you'll have disagreements, and you'll go through struggles together. But no matter what, don't ever leave her.

"The same goes for your kids. When you decide to have kids, you make an eternal commitment to them. You can *never* leave them.

"The worst kind of quitter is the kind who quits on his family. Don't *ever* do it." His voice got particularly loud when he stressed that point. He'd seen what a fatherless home could do to kids. Big Jim would've hated to see the increasing rate of fatherless homes these days—especially here in the Rust Belt.

"With every decision you make, you have to ask yourself, 'How will this affect my family?'

"Then, listen to that voice inside you. Follow your heart."

Big Jim turned back to the chalkboard and wrote:

NO. 3 – PASSION.

"Third on the list is passion. This means your job, what you decide to do for a living. You've got to find something you're truly passionate about and make that your life's work.

"Your ancestors didn't have the choices you have. They paved the way for you to live the American Dream. They had to do work they didn't like, but the sacrifices they made created the opportunity for you to do something you're passionate about. You owe it to them to follow that passion.

"Men, if you find something you love to do, make it your career. Don't chase money, don't chase power, and don't worry about fame and prestige. Find something you love to do and find a way to do that for a living.

"Find something that consumes you, something you can't stop thinking about. That's your passion talking. That's where you'll find the career you're meant to have. That's where you'll find your professional purpose.

"Understand that doing something you love doesn't mean it will always be easy. You'll have to work extremely hard at whatever you decide to do and it won't always be fun. But if you love it, you'll always find a way to overcome the difficult times. If you don't love it, you'll be tempted to quit anytime something doesn't go your way.

"The people that love what they do rise to the top. If you're not passionate about your work, you will get beat by someone who is. I guarantee it.

"Chase your biggest dreams. Pursue your deepest passions. God gave each of you very specific, unique passions and you're *supposed* to follow them!

"Chasing your passion won't always make you rich and it won't necessarily make you famous, but it will make you happy. It will make you a success. It will make you a better husband, a better father, and a better man. That, I can promise you."

Back to the chalkboard, Big Jim wrote down: *NO. 4 – HEALTH*.

"If you put God, family, and work that you love first, you'll go a long way towards living a healthy life. But you still have to make a commitment to good health.

"When some of you walk out these doors tonight, you'll be tempted to never again lift a weight or run a sprint. Don't fall to that temptation. Make being strong and healthy a priority in your life. If you don't, your quality of life will suffer a great deal.

"You need to be strong in body and mind. Bad eating, lack of exercise, high stress, and lack of sleep are the four biggest causes of poor health.

"When faced with important decisions, don't forget to ask yourself how it might impact your health. You'd be surprised how many life decisions can negatively affect your health. Don't apologize for making good health one of your five life priorities. It's not something you can put off until later. It needs to be a priority."

Big Jim added one final priority to the chalkboard: *NO. 5 – COMMUNITY.*

"Don't ever ignore the importance of your community.

"Some of you guys may stay in Kingstown your whole life, you'll be members of this parish, and your kids will go to this school. And some people will look down on you for that. They'll shake their heads and ask you why you never left your hometown. Don't listen to them. If your heart is here, be where your heart is and don't apologize for it.

"Some of you guys will join new towns and cities

far from here. If that's where your heart leads you, by all means go there! And once you're there, embrace your community. Become a part of it. Help your neighbors, help your parish, and help your city be the best it can be.

"Go where your heart leads you and remember that you need to be part of your community — wherever that community is.

"We live in a society that celebrates the individual. You'll be tempted to cut ties, to go your own way, to put up a wall between you and your neighbors. You'll be tempted to believe that these actions create freedom. Too many people think that being tied to a community takes away your freedom. They think it means conforming instead of *being yourself.*

"Don't fall for this lie.

"God made us to rely on each other and to be part of a community. We need each other to thrive. Don't turn your back on your neighbor. Make sacrifices for your neighbors. You'll never become the best version of yourself if you're not committed to helping your community."

Big Jim looked over us and smiled. He could see

us listening intently to every word. He knew he was getting through to us.

"Men, I've just outlined for you the secret to living your life to the fullest. Follow your heart and live by these five priorities. It will always be safe to follow your heart as long as you have your priorities straight.

"When faced with a decision, simply ask yourself these five questions:

"One, what does God want me to do?

"Two, how will this affect my family?

"Three, is this getting me closer to my professional purpose in life?

"Four, how will this affect my health?

"And five, will this make my community stronger and better?

"Those five questions in that order. Follow your heart. When you ask these questions, do whatever your heart tells you to do.

"If you follow your heart, you'll never go wrong. I promise you. You'll *never* go wrong."

10

With everything that was going on, how could I give that speech? How could I look my players in the eye and tell them if they followed their hearts and kept their priorities straight, they'd never go wrong?

How could I tell my players something *I* no longer believed?

I had done exactly what Big Jim told me to do. Not every guy who heard *The Senior Speech* followed the advice my dad laid out, but I did. I followed it like Gospel. I analyzed every important life decision in light of the five questions Big Jim advised.

And look where it got me.

I'm in my mid-fifties and everything I've worked my whole life for — this parish, this program, this town, my pension — all of it is about to be taken away from me.

Everything Big Jim and I had preached year after year with that famous *Senior Speech* was a lie.

You can't go wrong as long as you follow your heart? What a joke.

Do what God placed in your heart and you will find

happiness? If only that were true.

I'd bought into Big Jim's words and what did I have to show for it? The most state championship *losses* in history, a broken-down hometown, a bankrupt school, and an obliterated pension.

And look where all this had left my family?

I never had the money to help my kids out with college. My daughters would be loaded with debt when they graduated, just like my sons. Not like Andy's daughter, who would never be burdened with such things. She graduated from Harvard without owing a penny thanks to her father. Andy knew how to provide for his kid.

My youngest son, Micky, would now have to start at a new school, probably in a new town, right before his senior year. He'd have to leave his friends, his cousins, his girlfriend, and the community he'd always known.

My oldest son, Jimmy, who was a teacher and coach with me at St. Mary's, would now have to find a new place to call home. He and his wife just had a baby, a boy that Jimmy undoubtedly dreamed of coaching at St. Mary's someday. All those dreams he had about raising his kids here in Kingstown and coaching with me at St. Mary's for years to come vanished in an instant.

And how about me and Gina? We'd have to sell our house at a time when hundred-year-old homes in downtown Kingstown weren't exactly in high demand—and because we had refinanced our mortgage several times over the years to make ends meet, we probably wouldn't make enough to cover the down payment on a new house somewhere else. We'd have to find a new town to live in. We'd have to leave all our friends and family. I'd have to find a new job and Gina would have to go back to working fulltime. We'd be pretty much broke—losing everything we'd worked the last thirty years to build up and starting all over. I'd probably be working until the day I died.

Big Jim got off easy when that out-of-nowhere brain aneurysm took his life. He got to die instantly while doing something he loved, without seeing firsthand all the heartache that would come to Kingstown over the following decades. I'd have to spend the next twenty or thirty years digging and clawing just to get back to where I was...and quietly hoping that maybe an instant death might be lurking around the corner. At least then Gina and the kids could benefit from my life insurance policy.

Everything was gone.

We'd faced plenty of hard times in the past, but I always trusted my dad's words. I always believed that as long as I followed my heart and lived the purpose I believed God wanted me to live, we'd get through those hard times. It was a safety net, a sense of security that things would work out just as Big Jim had promised me it would.

But this was too much. This was the final straw.

I had followed my heart and look where it got me. Bitter, broke, and dreading my future.

Thanks, Dad. Thanks for your words of wisdom.

11

I was thinking crazy thoughts. I was panicking. I was despairing. I had to get out of the house—go for a walk and clear my head.

Gina stopped me before I headed out the front door.

"I can see the panic in your eyes," she said, placing her hand on my forehead. "I love you, John, and I promise you we will get through this. Pray, hope, and don't worry."

Gina was the strong one, I was the weak one. It had always been this way. I was quick to worry, quick to panic. She was the anchor. The one who trusted God's providence and believed everything would work out in the end. She was the one who, no matter what adversity we were facing, always told me everything would be alright.

But on this night—more so than any other time in my life—her words didn't bring me peace. None at all. In fact, they made me angrier.

How could you be so naïve? I thought to myself,

before saying curtly, "Thanks, hon, I won't be long."

I walked outside and started on my normal route towards Main Street. It was a windy night, but the brisk breeze was refreshing. I could again smell fireplaces burning and there was also that unmistakable smell of snow on the way. When I got to the corner at the end of our block, instead of taking a right and heading for Main Street, something stopped me.

Standing still, I looked up Oak Street to that tall church steeple with the cross on top and the statue of Mary about halfway up it glowing in the misty night. The church was calling me. Not in a peaceful, grace-filled, come-on-in-and-everything-will-be-okay kind of way. But in a bitter, how-the-hell-could-you-do-this-to-me kind of way. I wanted answers. And by God, I was going to get them straight from the source.

I stomped my way through the damp leaves that covered the sidewalk along Oak Street. With a grimace, I stormed past the grotto that marked the entrance to our campus. All those candles lit up in the grotto represented people's prayers — their hopes for a miracle. Each candle was a reminder that someone was praying for a sickness to be cured, a family to be protected, or a financial crisis to be averted. Undoubtedly, some of those candles represented prayers that our school would miraculously be saved. But I knew it didn't matter how many prayer candles were lit, nothing short of a winning lottery ticket would save our school and our jobs.

For a moment, I seriously considered heading up to the Quick Trip and buying a lottery ticket. Desperate times make us consider dumb solutions.

As I made my way up the steps to St. Mary's Church, I looked up at the steeple. I saw the statue of Mary above me—her outstretched arms indicating that we could always come to her with our problems and she would be there to watch over us, to intercede for us, to protect us. I huffed, shook my head, and opened one of the large wooden doors at the entrance of the church.

I half-expected to see the pews full of people kneeling in prayer, begging God for a miracle to save our school. Instead, there wasn't a single person inside. The place was deserted. Maybe no one really cared that much about this school. Or, maybe people had simply given up on the idea that prayer could make a difference. This was just another bad break on the long list of bad breaks to hit Kingstown, Ohio. Perhaps the people who had spent decades praying for their jobs and homes to be saved weren't going to waste any more time on their knees.

St. Mary's Church was one of those huge, ornate Catholic churches built in the early 1900s. The kind they don't build anymore. It was sturdy brick on the outside — making one believe that nothing could ever destroy it. The inside was beautiful — it could almost take your breath away the first time you saw it. Large, wide pillars ran up each side of the church. The huge dome above the altar was painted gold and blue. Elaborate stain-glass windows and holy statues portraying Christianity's most significant people and events were everywhere you looked. The smell of incense and wax candles overwhelmed you when you walked into this sacred place.

I walked up the center aisle, genuflected, and took a seat in the second-row pew. I sat there, looking up at the crucifix above the altar. The only sound was the howling wind outside and what I thought was a distant rumble of thunder — odd to have a thunderstorm this late in the year.

I turned my attention to the large stained-glass windows located behind and high above the altar. They portrayed Jesus and Mary, a white dove representing the Holy Spirit, and a dozen or so angels. Ever since I was a little kid, these beautiful images had brought me peace. They reminded me of the power of God and the importance of faith. They made me feel protected.

On this night, I looked up at these images and wondered how I didn't see this day coming.

What made you think you and your job were so special? I thought to myself. *What made you think God would save your school and your livelihood? Everything in Kingstown is on the way out. You've seen it all around you for decades now. What could possibly make you think that St. Mary's was safe?*

I had been offered other jobs through the years. Early in my coaching career, multiple other high schools had offered me better-paying jobs. A couple dozen times, I'd been asked to join a college staff. Four of those job offers, in particular, would have doubled my salary in an instant. Once, I was even offered an assistant job in the National Football

League—entry level, but definitely the start of a much better-paying path.

I hadn't received any new offers in the last fifteen years or so—probably because I was no longer considered a promising young coach, but was now thought of as an old-fashioned coach who couldn't adapt with the times *or* win the big game.

I seriously considered all those past offers. Each time, I decided it wasn't in my heart. Kingstown and St. Mary's High School was where my heart was. Just like Big Jim had always told me, I thought it was *safe* to follow my heart.

Were you following your heart or were you just afraid to try something different? I asked myself, echoing the question my brother Andy had hurled at me the last time we spoke to each other—about four years ago.

Whatever your reason was for staying here, you weren't using your head. You weren't paying attention to what was going on around you. And look where it got you.

It wasn't that I was angry at God; I was angry at myself for being so gullible and believing that God would protect me. I was angry at my dad for making me believe that if I just followed my heart and trusted God, everything would be alright.

How could I have been so stupid? How could I have relied on fairy tales and good intentions when making important life decisions? How could I have been so blind to reality?

At that moment, I heard a booming voice from behind me: "It's about time to end the pity party, don't you think?"

The voice startled me to the point that I actually leapt up from the pew. I turned around to see the unmistakable disjointed stride of the big, broad man I hadn't seen in twenty-nine years.

Walking briskly down the aisle with a hat in his hand and a half-grin on his face was my hero, my dad, Big Jim Callahan.

12

For as long as I could remember, Big Jim had always walked the same way: purposefully, like he was in a hurry, but also slowed down by a slight limp caused by an old knee injury. Funny, that's the first thing that stood out to me when I saw my long-deceased father walking towards me down the center aisle of St. Mary's Church. Do ghosts or angels or hallucinations—whatever this was—still have to contend with old football injuries? Apparently so.

"This can't be," I said, scared of what I was seeing. "I'm losing my mind."

"Hi, John," Big Jim said to me when he reached the second pew. He reached out with his right hand. I embraced it with mine and he pulled me in, wrapping his left arm around me. It was the way my dad had always hugged me, my brother, and my uncles. With my mom and sisters, it was always a normal hug; with men, it was always a half-handshake, half-hug.

His callused hand, his barrel chest, the smell of his

favorite cologne—my senses were overwhelmed by the physical *realness* of it all.

"You're real," I blurted out.

"Hell yes, I'm real," he said with a grin. He looked about the same age as he had been when he passed away, maybe a few years younger.

"But this can't be." I looked around the church to see if anyone else was seeing this. The place was empty except for the two of us.

"It can be, and it is," Big Jim said. "Consider yourself lucky. The Big Man doesn't allow for this kind of thing too often." When he said *Big Man* he nodded upward.

Fear finally gave way to joy and love. My eyes began to well with tears. All I could say was, "Dad."

I gave him a full hug and felt him pull me in tightly as I did.

"It's great to see you, son," he said before stepping back and gesturing for me to scoot down and make room for him on the pew. "I'm sorry to hear about St. Mary's shutting down. A real tragedy. I love this place. And I know you do too."

Big Jim sat down in the pew and I followed his lead.

"Is there anything you can do about it?" I asked.

Big Jim smiled. "Unfortunately, that's above my paygrade. The only supernatural power I've been granted is to be here, with you, to answer your questions."

My shoulders dropped and I couldn't hide my disappointment. I should have been overwhelmed with joy to see my father. What most people would give to have one more moment with a deceased parent. But here I was, focused only on the problems I was facing and not on the gift sitting next to me.

"Sorry to disappoint you," Big Jim said.

I rubbed my eyes. "This is all just…so surreal."

"It's real, I assure you, now let's not waste any more time repeating that fact. Let's get to why I'm here. You've got some questions for me and I guess God thinks you deserve some answers."

I nodded.

"Well, spit 'em out and don't hold back," he said, still delivering his sentences in the pre-snap-cadence-style I'd always remembered. "Now's not the time to sugarcoat your feelings. You've got a big game tomorrow and the sooner we can get your mind focused on that, the better."

Big Jim had always been in a hurry and apparently an eternal perspective hadn't changed that.

13

I started with the most pressing question on my mind. "I don't think I'm going to give *The Senior Speech* tomorrow. What do you think about that?"

"I think you should reconsider," Big Jim said without a moment's pause.

I wasn't the least bit surprised by his stance on the issue. "Dad, look at what's going on. Look at what's happening to these kids and to me. How can I tell them everything will work out for them as long as they follow their hearts?"

"I never said that life would be a breeze and you'd never face adversity as long as you followed your heart. I said that you'll never go wrong following your heart. I said it would always be better than the alternative. And I *still* say that."

"But that's just it," I said. "The alternative *would* have been better for me and my family. Following my heart got me to where I am right now, soon to be broke, unemployed, and without a home. Had I followed my head instead of my heart, I would've taken one of those better jobs. I would've gotten out of this dying town long ago and made a lot more money. Life would've been a lot easier."

"You really believe that?" Big Jim asked.

"How can I not? I'm broke, I'm unemployed…"

"…Yeah, yeah, yeah, you already said all that. Seriously, can you drop the self-pity? I raised you better than that."

That was the Big Jim I'd always known. The two things he always had little patience for were feeling sorry for yourself and making excuses. He used to say, "You can whine about it, you can complain about it, but eventually you need to figure out what the hell you're going to *do* about it!"

I nodded, still the obedient son who didn't want to disappoint his old man.

"Now look, you've been dealt a rough blow," Big Jim said. "I know it hurts, I know you're disappointed, and I know you're worried. But don't let your anger and worry cloud your judgment. What you have done over the last thirty years here has fulfilled your purpose—your life's mission up to this point—in more ways than you can imagine. You've had an impact on a lot of other people.

"It ain't all about you, ya' know?" This was another line from Big Jim we had heard constantly growing up.

"I realize that and I've never forgotten that," I said. "But let's be realistic, a lot of the lives I've affected haven't turned out so good."

"Is that so?" Big Jim asked.

"No doubt about it," I said, raising my voice.

He waited for me to give an example.

"Look at the most famous player to ever play for me," I said. "Look at what happened to Ricky Walsh."

14

What happened next is difficult to describe. I was still sitting next to my dad in the second pew at St. Mary's Church, but I suddenly saw a past moment in my life with such clarity it was almost as though I was watching a movie in my mind. This scene wasn't a cloudy vision from the past—like what you normally see in your mind when you revisit old memories. Instead, it was crystal clear. It was like Big Jim could project the scenes into my mind.

I wasn't physically taken to revisit the past, but I could watch the scene play out and then turn and talk to Big Jim, right there in the church, whenever I wanted.

The scene I saw, while sitting in that church next to my dad, was from eleven years ago almost to the day. My forty-two-year-old-self was sitting in my office at the school. Across the desk from me was Ricky Walsh.

I saw the 2005 version of me rubbing my forehead. I saw Ricky leaning back with a smile on his face. This was the Wednesday before the state championship game.

The most famous player to ever come out of St. Mary's High School, Ricky Walsh would become a Heisman Trophy winner, a No. 1 draft pick in the NFL, and one of the biggest flops in the history of professional sports.

But before he was those things, Ricky was the starting senior quarterback for my 2005 team.

Lots of seventeen-and-eighteen-year-olds have big egos. As anyone who has spent time in secondary education will tell you, it's common for a high school senior to have an unwarranted amount of confidence, a level of confidence that can come across as reckless and even rude. These kids are on top of the world at this moment in time. They think they have all the answers.

Ricky Walsh took that senior swagger to a whole new level.

He was one of the nation's top high school football recruits and he had his pick of scholarship offers from all of college football's top programs. He had been our starting quarterback since his sophomore season and I had redesigned my offense to cater to his skillset.

Throughout my coaching career, I had used the same run-first, triple-option offense that Big Jim had used, only slightly modified. That is — throughout my career except for the three years Ricky was my quarterback. For him, we converted to a shotgun spread offense that threw the ball often while also allowing Ricky to take off and run whenever he wanted.

Ricky had a cannon for an arm and the speed to play wide receiver if he wanted to. He was extremely competitive on Friday nights — the type of kid that would run head-first into a brick wall if he thought it would result in a victory.

I have never coached a more physically-gifted individual than Ricky Walsh.

The problem was that Ricky was well aware of this fact. He knew he had been blessed disproportionally by the football gods and in a football-crazed state like Ohio, that meant he had the world on a string. He thought he could do no wrong.

We butted heads for three long years. He knew how important he was to the team. He knew he could push the envelope. As much as I assured him he'd never get any special treatment from me, he'd always respond with a sly nod that said, "We'll see about that."

The struggle with Ricky was discipline. He'd go half-speed during sprints at the end of practice. He'd sometimes abruptly walk to the sidelines during practice and declare with a chuckle, "I need a break, Coach." He'd show up late to team meetings with one lame excuse after another. He didn't blatantly break team rules in these instances, but he pushed the envelope as far as he could push it.

As a football coach, you want your best players to be team leaders. You want them to be positive examples for the rest of the team. On Friday nights when the lights were on, Ricky had a competitive drive that lifted the whole team up and he put forth the type of never-back-down effort that *was* an extraordinary example for the rest of the team.

It was the other six days of the week where Ricky was a problem.

But on this day — the Wednesday before our 2005 state championship game — as Ricky sat across from me with that confident grin, I was faced with the toughest coaching decision of my career.

"Did you do it?" I asked him, not wanting to hear the answer.

"What do you want me to say, Coach?" Ricky said, still smiling, like this was all another big joke.

"I want you to tell me the truth."

I knew the truth. He knew I knew the truth. To be honest, part of me wanted him to lie to me. At least then I could hide behind the "I have to trust my players" rationalization.

"You really want the truth?" he said, challenging me.

I nodded. "The truth, Ricky."

"Yeah, I did it." For the first time, he dropped his smile, almost like he surprised himself with his admission. For the first time, he had the slightest look of nervousness on his face.

It was our final showdown. It was put-up-or-shut-up time. For three years, I had assured Ricky that he had to follow our team's rules just like everyone else. And for three years, he had tested me without ever actually crossing the line—or at least *admitting* that he had.

Now, he told me point-blank that he had indeed broken one of our team's rules. He had broken our school's honor code. Ricky had been seen drinking alcohol at a party following last Friday's state-semifinal victory. Our school and team policy was clear on the matter: if a student-athlete is caught drinking, he or she shall be suspended for the following game on a first offense, and for the entire season on a second offense. It didn't matter if that next game was potentially the final game of the season. If a student-athlete broke the rule, they didn't play.

I was told about the incident Tuesday night. Obviously, there was a part of me that wanted to ignore the complaint. But I told myself I had a moral obligation to confront Ricky about it. I called him into my office moments before our Wednesday practice. And now, here he was, admitting that it was true.

He could've lied. He could've claimed he would never do such a thing, that he was home sleeping after a tough game. He could do those things with a knowing nod and a smirk on his face.

But, he chose to tell the truth. I had to admire that, at least.

I also knew he was challenging me to follow

through on what I said I would do. All the chips were on the table. Which one of us would budge? Not him; he told the truth. It was now my turn.

I closed my eyes, leaned back in my desk chair, and exhaled. "You know what this means, Ricky."

"I don't think I do, Coach. Why don't you tell me?"

I opened my eyes. He wasn't smiling. He was glaring at me, with a hint of panic. I could see that he now regretted his decision to tell me the truth—though I doubted he had any regret for violating the school's honor code in the first place.

"You can't play on Saturday," I said. "You're sitting. You're done. Your season is over."

His jaw dropped. Almost instantly, I saw his eyes get watery.

But that was just for an instant. He quickly gathered himself back into too-cool mode. He leaned back and forced a smile.

"Okay, this is that part where I tell you I'll do anything you want me to do, right?" Ricky said. "You win. I'll write a five-thousand-word essay on the dangers of underage drinking. I'll run gassers until I puke. I'll do a hundred hours of community service. Just tell me what I need to do to play, Coach."

"I can't do it. This is a school rule with clear consequences. You knew it. You broke it. Now you have to pay the price."

Ricky's face reddened. "This is how you want to play it? This is your big soapbox moment, huh? This is your ego trying to put me in my place, is that it?"

"Nothing could be further from the truth, Ricky."

"Then don't do this."

"I don't have a choice," I said.

"Of course, you do!" Ricky stood up and was shouting now. "You're the head coach. You make these decisions. It's your choice. You can choose some other type of punishment for me. It's *your* choice!"

"No, Ricky, it was your choice. You knew the consequences and you did it anyway. You made the choice, not me."

Ricky's rageful eyes gave way to tears. The unbreakable Ricky Walsh was breaking down. The All-American quarterback was still just a 17-year-old kid from a broken home.

"So, what, is this supposed to be some life lesson

for me?" he said. "You're going to take away this game, tell all my recruiters what a bad kid I am, try to get my scholarships pulled so that I'm stuck living in this dive of a town just like you? Is that it?"

"Nobody's going to pull your scholarship offers," I said. "I'll make sure of that."

"There has to be *something* we can do. I need this game on Saturday. *We* need this game."

As the present-day me watched this scene from the past play out, my heart went out to Ricky. I had replayed this moment in my mind often throughout the years, questioning whether there was a better way I could have handled it, but I forgot how genuinely crushed Ricky had been. He was a troubled kid, he had to deal with a lot of tough issues at home, but playing football brought him pure joy. It was his escape in life. It was the one thing that made him feel special. It was the most precious thing in his life. And the biggest game of his life—up to that point—was now being taken away from him.

"I'm sorry, Ricky. There's no way out of this."

And with that, Ricky swatted over the lamp on my desk. It shattered violently when it hit the ground.

"What you're doing isn't right," he said to me, tears running down his face. "You know it isn't right. I wasn't the only player drinking that night and you know it."

"Tell me who else was and they're gone too."

Ricky shook his head. "No. No way. I'm a man of character. I won't rat on my friends. I won't turn my back on the people who count on me. I'm not like *you*."

And with that, Ricky stormed out of my office.

He never again put on a Panther uniform.

15

"Do you regret your decision?" Big Jim asked me, snapping me back to the present moment sitting in the church pew.

"I do," I said. "You always told me that you can't treat each player the same because each player *isn't* the same. Good coaches recognize this."

"When I said that, I was referring to teaching and motivating. Some kids respond best to a kick in the butt; they need to be challenged to rise to the occasion. Others back down and play scared if they're criticized; they need to be motivated only with positive reinforcement. Good coaches have to recognize those differences. I *never* meant that team rules should apply to some players, but not to others."

"But that kid, Ricky, I can't help but think I screwed him up for the rest of his life," I said. "He needed me to have his back. Ricky's dad walked out on the family when he was five or six. Ricky's mom was an alcoholic. His older brother was addicted to drugs, always in and out of jail. Ricky had no positive adult figures in his life. For once, he needed someone like me to say, 'Yes, you screwed up, but I've got your back, I won't abandon you.'"

"You think letting him break a team rule without suffering the consequences would have shown him he wasn't being abandoned?"

"Yes!" I said. "You watched that scene play out, Ricky was devastated. He felt betrayed…by *me*."

"And you lost the game on Saturday," Big Jim said.

"That's not what this is about."

"You sure?"

I looked away. He knew and I knew that some of the regret I felt about not allowing Ricky to play in the championship game was due to the fact that we lost that game. The community couldn't believe I had done it. I heard the talk. Some people said I was putting *my* authoritative ego above what was best for the team. They said I needed to adapt with the times and recognize that kids will be kids.

The decision has haunted me for years.

"My regret goes beyond the game," I said. "Sure, I know we would've won had Ricky played for us, but

I also look at what happened to Ricky after that. Look at all the poor choices he has made since. He didn't learn a thing from that incident except that he was all alone in this world—abandoned in his moment of need."

After the state championship loss in 2005, I spent the next two weeks assuring every college recruiter that Ricky was a good kid who simply made a poor decision.

"He's from a tough home and needs a little more discipline," I told the recruiters. "But, when push came to shove, he stood up and told the truth about what he had done. That showed a lot of character."

Not a single scholarship offer was pulled.

Ricky committed to Cal State and after a redshirt season, he was a two-year starter. He won the Heisman Trophy as the best college football player in the country in 2008. He left college early to enter the NFL and despite rumors about "character issues" prior to the draft, Ricky was the NFL's No. 1 draft pick the following spring. He signed a six-year deal worth $80 million ($60 million guaranteed).

And that was the highlight of his professional career. Everything went downhill after Draft Day.

He spent most of the summer before his rookie season in Las Vegas. Ricky's excessive partying was notorious before he ever took a snap in the NFL. He started eight games as a rookie in 2009. He threw twelve interceptions and just four touchdown passes in those eight games.

He was arrested in the spring of 2010 for possession of narcotics. He went to rehab in the summer, but fell back to his hard-partying ways as soon as he was out.

By the end of the 2010 season, he had been benched. In 2011, he was traded, but never saw the field. He was arrested again that December on charges of possession and disorderly conduct.

By 2012, no NFL team would touch him and his football career was over.

Through it all, Ricky made many enemies back in Kingstown. While at Cal State, he made several public references to how awful his hometown was and how he'd never go back.

During an ESPN interview prior to his rookie season in the NFL, his childhood came up. He told the reporter, "My hometown, Kingstown, it's the armpit of America. Seriously, it's a rusted-out

Podunk town full of judgmental people longing for the good old days. To all those people back there who didn't think I'd ever amount to anything, how do you like me now?" He smiled smugly into the camera and broke the hearts of many Kingstown residents.

Kingstown's most famous patron blasted the town and the community as publicly as he possibly could.

By the end of his short-lived career, Ricky Walsh represented yet another major disappointment for the city of Kingstown, Ohio.

16

"And you think things would have turned out differently for Ricky if you had allowed him to skirt the rules when he played for you?" Big Jim asked.

"He obviously didn't learn anything positive from the situation," I said.

"I think you'll find that, ultimately, you did the right thing."

"You think I made the right decision?"

"I do," Big Jim said.

Hearing my dad, my hero, say that he agreed with my decision—all these years later—was like a huge weight being lifted off my shoulders. Like most of my life decisions, I always wondered what my dad would've done in the same circumstances. I still wasn't sure my handling of the Ricky Walsh situation was the best thing for everyone involved, but the fact that Big Jim approved of what I had done removed a lot of the guilt I'd carried with me over the years.

Momentarily.

Then, I remembered who I was talking to. Big Jim was as "old school" as an old-school coach can be. No matter how much I still tried to do things the way Big Jim had, I saw the world around me changing and I questioned whether his old-fashioned ways of doing things were still valid. Was being "old school" just another way to say that one is stubborn and unwilling to change with the times? Was trying to do everything the way Big Jim had done them the reason I kept losing state championships, the reason I never took better job opportunities, and the reason people like Ricky Walsh bashed this town and never came back as soon as they left it?

"Of course, *you* agree with what I did," I said to Big Jim. "And that's the problem. I've been trying to do things the way you taught me to do them for the last thirty years and…"

I stopped myself.

"And what?" Big Jim asked.

"And look where it's gotten me. Look where it got Ricky. Look where it got this town, this school, everything."

"John, your decision had a tremendous impact on every single player on that team. They all saw that there were consequences to their decisions. They saw that nobody—not even the great Ricky Walsh—was above the rules. And frankly, the last thing Ricky needed was someone telling him he could do whatever he wanted and still be successful. Obviously, that's the message he received all through college and things didn't turn out so well for him after that."

"But maybe if he hadn't felt so abandoned by me, he would've followed a different path," I said. "His partying, his drug use—it's all such an obvious cry for help.

"The world has changed since your days of coaching, Dad. I blame myself for not seeing this sooner. Kids have changed and I've failed to adapt."

With that, Big Jim leaned back with a laugh and shook his head. "Don't even *try* to pull that one," he said. "Kids haven't changed a bit. It's the adults who have changed. It's the adults who have set lower standards for kids. It's the adults who try to make everything easier on the kids. It's the adults who don't hold kids accountable for their decisions, their manners, and their values. But when adults do that, what are we setting up the kids for? For failure, that's what.

"If you lower your expectations and try to make everything so easy on the kids, they'll quit at the first sign of trouble once they get into the real world. If you let one kid break the rules, you're a hypocrite. And if you get rid of the rules altogether—try to make everything easy on the kids, give them all second, third, and fourth chances—you're stuck with a bunch of kids who never have any discipline, kids who never take any responsibility, and kids who never learn right from wrong.

"Kids haven't changed a bit. They'll respond to the expectations that are set for them, just like they always have. It's the adults—the parents, the teachers, and the coaches—who have changed.

"The fact that you're even questioning whether you made the right decision with Ricky shows you how much expectations have been lowered these days.

"You did the right thing, John. No doubt about it."

For thirty years, I had taught, coached, and lived by the old-school code Big Jim had taught me. I had emphasized doing the right thing, putting character first, and setting high expectations for my students and players. Whether my dad was right or not, hearing that he approved of the way I had chosen to do things gave me a confidence boost. It made me proud. For a moment, I stopped thinking about all the things that were going wrong around me and a thought entered my head: *at least I did things the right way while I was here*.

"You may find this hard to believe, but you made a more positive impact on Ricky than you realize," Big Jim said. "His life isn't over. Far from it. He knows he needs to turn things around and he thinks about you often. He may not be ready to admit it yet, but he's starting to understand that if he had listened to all those lessons you taught him, his playing career would've turned out much better. Ricky's story isn't over with; he's still got a lot of life left."

Ricky had avoided making headlines over the last few years. I'd heard rumors that he lived in Las Vegas and had blown all his money partying, gambling, and drinking. His mother passed away not too long after he left for college. His brother was in prison. There were no more Walsh family members left in Kingstown.

I hoped Big Jim was right and that Ricky would turn his life around before it was too late.

17

"John, you worry too much," Big Jim said. "You always did. You can't dwell on one player and one decision. You made your decision, you made the best decision you could make, and you made the exact same decision I would've made. It's over and done with. You have to move on knowing that regardless of how things turned out, you did the right thing with the information you had."

Big Jim may not have had the power to save my job or this school, but he did still have the awesome fatherly power to make his son feel better about himself.

"Every coach and teacher is going to have some kids that don't buy into the message." Big Jim said. "It's sad, but it's part of the job. You can't let the bad apples spoil the bunch.

"Ricky Walsh may not have turned out a model citizen, but you've had a positive impact on hundreds of others. You don't see the big picture, but the lessons you've taught have helped your former players and students persevere through life's toughest times. Your former players have had to bounce back from lost jobs, from troubled relationships, and from health crises. The lessons you taught them about building grit, about persevering, about never backing down, about taking responsibility for their choices—those lessons drove them forward through their toughest times.

"And they've passed those lessons on to others. It's a ripple effect that reaches so much further than you can imagine.

"Son, they can shut down this school and they can take a wrecking ball to this entire town, but the positive lessons you and I taught here will never die. They'll live on for generations to come."

I knew Big Jim was right. But it didn't make the current situation any less painful.

"But where is the justice?" I asked. "If we did things the right way and taught such valuable lessons, why aren't things working out for this town and this school? Why isn't all that faith, hope, and hard work being rewarded? Why doesn't God protect this place so we can *continue* to teach these lessons?"

"That I can't answer," Big Jim said. "All I know for certain is that the values you and I taught here have made communities stronger. The priorities we emphasized have kept families together."

Hearing the words *community* and *family* triggered a rush of bitterness back to the forefront of my mind.

"A lot of good it's done for *my* community and *my* family," I said.

18

At that instant, I saw another vivid image of a past moment in my life. I was sitting in a booth at Bob's Diner. We had a booth by the window and wintry flurries fell outside. Across the table from me was Mike Murphy. The two of us both looked twenty years younger.

"Do you remember this?" I heard Big Jim say, almost like the narrator talking over a movie scene.

"Not really," I said.

"It was 1998, a week before Christmas," Big Jim said. "Mike Murphy asked you to meet him for coffee after a basketball game up at the school."

Mike was fifteen years older than me. He was the owner of Victory Sportswear, a clothing company located here in Kingstown. Mike's grandfather had started the company back in the 1940s and Mike had taken it over when his dad retired in the early 1990s.

Mike was a proud supporter of the school and the parish. He and I had become friends and we met for dinner or coffee dozens of times throughout the years—just as I met with so many other friends, supporters, and parents. These little meetings were a regular part of my life. This particular meeting didn't stand out as any more significant than the hundreds of others I've had over the years.

I now watched the scene play out.

"I want you to know, I'm still behind you," Mike said.

"Thank you, that really means a lot to me," I said, stirring my coffee.

"I mean it, when the school board meets next month, you've got my full support. I'm backing you one hundred percent."

I remembered now that this conversation was occurring right after my worst season as a head coach. In 1998, our team went 6-4 and missed the playoffs. I had come home after our final game of the regular season, a loss to Madison Heights, to find six FOR SALE signs planted in my front yard. As if I didn't already know that I had failed to meet expectations, some overzealous "fans" wanted to make sure I got the message.

"I appreciate that," I said to Mike. "I'm going to need all the help I can get on this one."

Watching the scene now, I was reminded how worried I had been at the time. In that diner, I saw that my shoulders were tense and I had bags under my eyes. That offseason was the closest I'd ever been to being fired from the job I loved. People were speculating that the game had passed me by and it was time for the school to find a new coach.

It's hard to believe when I look back on it. I was *thirty-five* at the time and people were saying I was too set in my ways—too "old fashioned" to lead this team.

"John, don't worry about it," I heard Mike say. "I can see you're stressed out about this. But listen, anyone who knows football knows this team is a year away from something big. I will do everything in my power to ensure you're back here next year and for years to come."

I nodded in appreciation. "You're a good friend, Mike."

Mike's prediction turned out to be correct. I would end up holding onto my job and we'd take an undefeated record into the state championship the following season. Of course, like every other time I made it that far, we would lose that state championship game.

"How's everything going for you?" I asked him.

"Actually, it's interesting you should ask. We're getting squeezed pretty hard at the moment. We just can't compete with those bigger companies who have all their gear made overseas for pennies on the dollar."

"I could see that," I said. "It doesn't seem fair."

"No, it doesn't. But, I have a solution—something that could get us out of trouble."

"Yeah?" I asked, genuinely curious as to how he would avoid the fate that had crushed so many other companies that actually *made things* in this part of the country.

"B&G Sporting Goods wants to partner up with us. They're offering big bucks to come in and help us out, help us cut costs, improve efficiency, all those things. And between you and me, their offer would set us up...well, for life."

"I don't understand. They want to pay you a fortune *and* help you out?"

Mike forced a smile as he shifted in his seat. I could see my question made him uncomfortable. "Well, they want to partner up with me. Take Victory

Sportswear to the next level."

"They want to partner up with you or they want to buy you out?"

More uneasiness. "We'd be partners," Mike said. "I'd still own part of the company."

"Who would own the majority?"

Mike looked down at his coffee. "They'd be majority owners." Then he looked back up at me. "But it's an amazing deal. Like I said, it would set us up for life."

I smiled. "You mean it would set *you* up for life, right?"

Mike didn't respond. He didn't like me asking that question. And, watching this scene play out nearly twenty years later, I didn't blame him. It really wasn't my place to tell him how he should handle *his* business.

"I'm not judging you, Mike," I said, trying to ease the tension I'd caused. "I think it's great how your family has been able to keep Victory alive through the years and keep it growing. And if this is the end game, if this is the payday you've been waiting for, I'm happy for you."

"Yeah?" he asked.

"Absolutely," I said.

"I appreciate that," Mike said as he exhaled, relieved. "I'm glad to hear you say that. Your opinion means a lot to me."

"But, you and I both know how this ends."

Mike tensed up again and tilted his head to the side as if to ask, *what do you mean?*

"You'll no longer have control of the company," I said. "B&G will. They'll come in and slash costs to make you more efficient. I assume that means improving your technology, getting you better wholesale prices on material, and helping you negotiate deals with schools, teams, and retail stores all over the country. All those things are great.

"But, in a few years, maybe less, they'll say they have to take more drastic measures to compete. At that point, cutting costs will mean cutting jobs. It will eventually mean shutting down your factory here and moving it overseas. The people of Kingstown will lose their jobs. People who have worked for Victory for decades will lose their jobs."

Mike looked at me in silence.

"Am I right?" I asked.

He looked down at his coffee again. "I hope it

doesn't come to that, I really do."

"Mike, am I right?"

Another moment of silence as he looked up at me.

"Don't make me out to be one of those greedy corporate raiders or something," Mike finally said. "I didn't take over this company to flip it and make myself a millionaire. But this is a family business. We're just barely hanging on. We don't have much of a choice. If we don't take this deal, we could be closed down in a year or two anyway. This buyout—this is a golden opportunity for us. This buyout is what success looks like for us."

"This is a family town," I said. "We're all just barely hanging on. And the jobs you're providing right now is what success looks like to those who work for you."

Mike huffed. "You obviously don't think I should do it."

"I'm not a businessman and I don't know all the details. I don't know what your purpose is. But to me, if you want to pass the company on to your kids and if you want to continue to be one of the top job providers right here in Kingstown, then you can't sell out to B&G."

"But this company will fail if I don't," Mike said.

I held up one finger. "One, what does God want you to do?"

I held up two fingers. "Two, how will this affect your family?"

I continued to count off the five questions Big Jim had taught us all through the years. "Three, is this getting you closer to your professional purpose in life?

"Four, how will this affect your health?

"And five," I paused for a moment. "Will this help or hurt your community?"

Mike leaned back and put his hands behind his head. "You just had to go there, didn't you?"

19

"Now do you remember that conversation?" Big Jim asked me, back in the church pew.

I nodded. I also remembered that 1998 wasn't the only time Mike had stood up for me when my job was in jeopardy.

"I hadn't thought about that night in years," I said. "Mike's a good friend. I owe him a lot. He always had my back. He was always there for me."

"And you were there for him as well."

"I remember thinking that I offended him that night. I walked home thinking I had just upset one of the few people trying to *save* my job. Who the hell was I to tell him how to run his business?"

"He *was* offended…at first…because you didn't tell him what he wanted to hear. But, he knew you were right. In the weeks after your conversation, he couldn't get your words and those five questions out of his head. And you know what happened after that."

"I know he didn't sell out and he kept the

company going. It's still here in Kingstown, still one of the town's largest employers."

"Mike gave up a lot of money in that deal," Big Jim said. "But, he found a way to turn the corner with his company. He realized being able to proudly display 'MADE IN THE U.S.A.' on all their gear was not only great for the people of Kingstown, but it was great marketing for his brand. His biggest competitors couldn't put that on their labels."

"You're making it sound like our little conversation was the reason he didn't take the deal," I said. "But I'm sure there were other factors. I heard that the offer from B&G fell through."

"It did," Big Jim said. "But the reason it fell through was because Mike refused to sell without assurance that the factory and the jobs would stay in Kingstown. Your opinion meant something to him. He needed someone like you to remind him what selling out would do to the community."

"I honestly didn't think much about that little conversation. I was so worried about my job at the time."

"It's the little things that make such a big difference in life."

I looked into my dad's eyes and saw the slightest hint of a tear. Big Jim never showed much emotion. I never once saw him cry.

"Those are the things that matter, son. Those little things make a big difference. They make a difference in so many other lives. I'm prouder of you for that one conversation, for saying what you believed in your heart in that one moment, than I could ever be about you winning a football game — championship or not.

"Success isn't about how many games you win or how much prestige you attain. Winning a state championship has *nothing* to do with your true legacy. What matters most are the lessons you teach, the impact you have on your community, and the types of men your players eventually become.

"Had you not been there with Mike — in that moment — had you not been honest and stuck to your values — in that moment — well, who knows what would've happened to Victory and all its employees. All those employees and their families."

There it was again. The word *family* bit me when Big Jim said it.

"I'm glad I could help *those* families," I said. "Too

bad I've let my own family down."

20

"What do you mean by that?" Big Jim asked me. "You've got four wonderful kids and Gina—could you have ever hoped for a better wife?"

"That's what I mean," I said. "They're all great and I've let them down. They deserve better."

"How did *you* let them down? You're not the reason the school is closing. And people have to relocate and find new jobs all the time. You're tough and you've raised a tough family. You will all be fine."

"Dad, I've lost *everything*. My pension is gone, our house will be gone. Everything I've given my whole life to, everything my family has always known—it's *all* being ripped away from us. I'm so mad at myself for thinking that things would work out if I just 'followed my heart.'" I made air quotes when I said *follow my heart*, mocking my father's famous words.

"Your fears about the future are causing you to forget all the good things the past has given you," Big Jim said. "You raised your kids in this town, at this school. You'll always have that. So Micky will have to attend another high school for one year, maybe it will be good for him. He's a tough kid, he can handle it. Be thankful for what this place has given you all these years.

"Don't let your fears about what *might* happen in the future cloud your memories of what did happen in the past."

I shook my head. "You don't get it, Dad. Things have changed. The way you did things—the way I keep telling my kids and my players and my students to *continue* doing things—those ways don't work anymore. This whole situation is more proof of that. Everything has changed.

"Things aren't like the way they used to be. You always said that St. Mary's was a family. You always pushed the importance of family and community—of sticking together and helping out one another when times get tough. But nobody buys into that anymore. It's every man for himself. People grow up here, they move out, and they don't *ever* come back.

"Me living here—just like you did—and my kids living here—just like I did—people don't do that anymore. Trying to do it that way only sets everyone up for disappointment and struggle. Guys like me and Alonzo—committing our lives to this school, this town, this parish—it has only set us up for disaster. What do we have to show for it? A bankrupt school, a vanished retirement, six state championship *losses*, and a future doing God-knows-what for the next thirty years.

"Andy did it the right way," I said, referring to my younger brother. "He was the smart Callahan. He got out of this town when he had the chance and he never looked back. He went out and made a real *living* for himself. He doesn't have to worry about pensions or college debt or school closings. He takes care of his daughter and gives her everything she wants. He doesn't have a care in the world except where he'll take his next vacation. He took control of his life and now he's living the dream.

"And can you believe how much I used to judge him? Can you believe I made jokes about how shallow his life was and how spoiled his daughter was? Who's laughing now? He was right and I was wrong. He had the courage to leave this place and make his own way. I had the chance and I blew it."

My dad let me finish my rant. Then, after a

moment of sitting in silence, he smiled and said, "I'm glad to finally hear you saying something nice about your brother."

I didn't smile back.

"I love both of you boys very much," Big Jim said. "And I've watched both of you try to make the best decisions you could for your lives. But you know better than to think Andy lives a carefree existence. He's made plenty of mistakes and he knows it. He's stressed out just as much as the next guy. Andy may be wealthy, but in many ways, his life is much more difficult than yours. You may be shocked to hear this, but many times Andy finds himself wishing he had *your* life. He hasn't always followed his heart—he knows it—and he's lived with the consequence."

"I wish I lived with those types of consequences."

Big Jim gave my sarcastic remark a courtesy chuckle. "Whether it's Andy, your sisters, or anyone else, don't get in the habit of comparing yourself to others. Petty jealousy doesn't do you any good." His tone turned more serious now. "*Everybody* has problems—problems you can't begin to imagine. Whining about how much better someone else has it than you is what a spoiled child does. I raised you better than that."

His words stung. Just as much as they did when I *was* a child.

"The most disappointing thing I've seen happen since I left this world is seeing my sons, my two boys, stop talking to each other," Big Jim said. "Family is a bond that should never be broken and you two have broken it. I pray every day that you and Andy will make amends."

21

Once again, it was as though Big Jim had flipped a switch and turned on a movie in my mind. This particular scene I remembered all too well. I had replayed it often in my mind over the last four years.

Of course, as we all tend to do, my memory of what had been said during this argument with my brother changed over the years. We remember the offensive things someone said to us, but we forget the offensive things we said to them. Seeing the replay now, I saw it as it actually happened.

I'm embarrassed to admit that while I had held onto and rehashed all the ugly things Andy had said to me that night, I had conveniently forgotten the awful things I had said to my brother.

It was the day after Christmas, 2012—nearly four years ago. Andy, his daughter, Claire, and his second wife, Allison, had come to visit for a few days over Christmas break. (Andy and Allison would divorce the following year.) It had been a somewhat-tense holiday visit up to this moment and the three of them were heading out the next day.

Andy and I were alone on my back deck. We had just finished eating the steaks I had grilled up for everyone. The frigid late-December air never stopped me from breaking out the grill at least once a week — even in the winter — and now Andy and I were enjoying a couple post-meal beers.

"John, those steaks were outstanding," Andy said. "That's something I never do — grill my own food. It seems like every meal I eat these days is at a five-star restaurant and, let me tell you, I'd choose one of your steaks over half the stuff I eat."

"Thanks…I guess," I said.

"You know what I mean," Andy said with a laugh.

I held my tongue and tried to force something nice. "It's been nice seeing you, Andy, I wish you all could stay longer."

Andy laughed again, as though I'd just made a hilarious joke. "Claire wants to be in Times Square for the ball drop on New Year's Eve. Before that, Allison wants to spend some time at the house in Palm Beach. Besides, four days is about all I can handle back in Kingstown."

I rolled my eyes. "Is it really that awful here, little brother?"

"I didn't mean it like that," Andy said.

I should've let it go right then. After four days of family reunion time, a little tension is bound to build up. As many families do, we had a tendency to laugh off each other's snide comments in the moment and then stew about them later.

But I didn't let it go this time.

After a moment of uncomfortable silence, I asked, "What *did* you mean?"

"I just meant...well...that it's been a nice time, but I'm ready to get back home. Hell, I was ready two days ago."

"You always have to do that, don't you?" I said. "You always have to put us down."

"I'm not putting *you* down," Andy said. "If I was you, I would probably never want to leave this place, either. You're a god here. You're a national-championship-winning quarterback, the second coming of Big Jim himself. I can see why *you* love this place. But for guys like me, this place isn't so kind. I can't stay here more than a day or two before it starts to bring me down."

"And what exactly makes this such a horrible place for *guys like you*?"

"You really want to have this conversation?" Andy asked.

"You've started it several times over the last few days, let's finish it," I said.

"Started what?"

"You know what I'm talking about. All the smirks when I say something about my team—I know you think it's silly how seriously people take sports around here. I see the mocking grins you and Allison share whenever we talk about a new shop or restaurant opening up downtown—like it's all so cute in our small-town, Podunk way. You've mentioned at least ten times that you can't *believe* so-and-so still lives here."

"John, take it easy. I'm just joking around with my brother. I thought you had a sense of humor."

"After a while, it doesn't seem like a joke," I said. "This place may be a dive to people *like you*, but it's our community. It's part of who we are. And when you insult us right and left, it gets offensive."

Andy put up his hands in a calm-down motion.

"Let's hear it," I said. "Tell me who *people like you*

are and why you could never live in a place like Kingstown."

"You really want to hear it?"

I nodded.

"I know this makes me sound like an arrogant S.O.B., but let's just say that someone like me is...well...*ambitious*." Andy said. "I want more out of life. I'm someone who has interests besides who's returning next year on a small-town high school football team and what the Kingstown City Council is planning for next spring. My life means more than who won Friday night's football game, which is all you people ever talk about. I want to eat at nice restaurants, I want to travel the world, and, yes, I want to make millions of dollars. Is that so wrong? I want to push myself and reach my full potential. I want to live life to the fullest!"

"You think I'm not ambitious because I became a football coach?"

"No, absolutely not. A football coach can be ambitious. I know lots of football coaches who are ambitious. But guess what? They don't stay in the same small town their whole life. They work their way up the ranks. They become college and pro coaches. They push themselves as far as they can. They're not afraid to see how far they can go."

"I've had offers for the next level," I said.

"I know you have—and that's exactly my point! You turned them down because you were too afraid to leave Kingstown."

"I turned them down because I didn't want those jobs," I said. "I didn't have the desire to coach in college or the NFL. My heart told me to stay here."

"Spare me the senior speech, dad," Andy said in a mocking tone. "If I had followed *my heart*, I'd probably be in bar band somewhere making a hundred bucks a week." Andy always loved music and he had been in a pretty good rock band during his high school and college days.

"Maybe not," I said. "If you loved it, you should've kept doing it. Who knows how far you could've gone. If you weren't still in a band, maybe you'd be a producer or something, making your living in music, doing what you love. And who knows how much happier you'd be."

"Who says I'm not happy?"

"You do. You told me two days ago that your *second* marriage is already falling apart and that you barely know your own daughter. And the constant bragging you do about all the money you make, all the possessions you have, and all the people you know is a pathetic attempt to cover up your sadness."

"I didn't realize you were a therapist now," Andy said. "Just because I didn't stay in this dump of a town and coach at the same dinky school as you and Dad doesn't mean I hate my life. In fact, I can't *imagine* living here."

"You've made your feelings about Kingstown clear," I said. "But I'm not talking about where you live; I'm talking about what you do. You make your living taking over companies that don't want to be taken over and then shutting down their factories and firing their workers."

"That's a low blow, John. That's a very small part of my job."

"Whatever it is you do, you told me yourself that you hate it. I just think you should've followed your heart like Dad always told us to do."

"This is exactly the problem with all that *follow-your-heart* advice. Follow your heart and everything will be okay? Give me a break. It's more like follow your heart and you'll end up broke, asking your little brother to help you with your mortgage."

That one stung and I felt angry blood rush into my face. "You had to go there, didn't you?"

Andy took a step back. He realized he had crossed a line. "Look, I'm happy to help you out—I really am. All I'm saying is that maybe if you had taken a look at life outside of Kingstown you could've made it big-time in the coaching world. You wouldn't have to live in an old house two doors down from where we grew up. You wouldn't have to worry about money all the time. You could send your kids to whatever college they wanted and help them out when they needed it. But you never even tried to make it big. You never even challenged yourself."

"You don't think being a teacher and coach is a challenging profession?" I asked. "You think I like being underpaid for the hours I put in? You think I enjoy all the stress that comes with coaching a team that expects nothing less than an undefeated state championship every season?

"I'm here *despite* the challenge. It's the most fulfilling challenge I can imagine. It's what I was born to do."

Andy laughed at me. "John, who are you kidding? You're here because you want to be like Dad and because you didn't have the courage to ever try anything new."

"I'm here because I believe it's where I'm supposed to be," I said. "I'm here because I believe it's my God-given purpose in life."

"So, God gave you this purpose, huh? Too bad He didn't also give you the income you need, isn't it? At the very least, he could have shown you how to win a state title by now, couldn't He?"

My face was red, my blood was boiling, and my voice was rising. "I'd rather be here, doing exactly what I'm doing, than to become the shallow, self-centered, philandering, egotistical ass you have become."

"Oh, *I'm* the one with the ego, huh?" Andy looked down and shook his head. "You're the one always acting high and mighty, like you're the moral compass above everyone else. Who crowned you the king of right and wrong? And stop taking about my personal life, you don't know half the story. Allison hasn't exactly been faithful in this marriage either."

"You cheating on your wife represents everything

else about you," I said. "It's like you're purposely rebelling against everything Mom and Dad and the Church always taught us. It's like you're trying to prove that you don't need to live by their rules or their morals. And look where it's gotten you. You only care about yourself and what you want. You don't care about who you hurt when you cheat on your wife and you don't care about the jobs you cut every time your company raids another business. It's all about how much fun *you* can have and how much money *you* can make."

Andy gave me a smug, *you-can't-be-serious* look. "You sure didn't have a problem with me or what I was doing with my life when you asked for that handout last summer, did you?"

"I think it's time you leave," I said. "Before I do something I might regret."

"You're asking me to leave this rickety old house in this dump of a town so that I can hop on a jet and go back to my mansion in Palm Beach?" Andy said, laying the sarcasm on thick. "How could you suggest something so cruel?"

I clenched my right hand into a fist. I barely stopped myself from taking a swing at my little brother.

Andy looked down and noticed my tightened fist.

"You seriously want to punch me, don't you?" he said, shaking his head. "You're pathetic, you know that? You're as pathetic as this whole town is."

"I don't want you around me and I don't want you around my kids," I said, with spite in my voice. "Get the hell out of here and don't ever come back."

"With pleasure," Andy said.

He stomped a few steps towards the back door and stopped. He turned around and said, "I hope you finally win a state title and prove to the world how great you are — or, at least prove it to the twenty people who actually give a crap about such things."

And with that, Andy walked back inside, gathered his wife and daughter, and left. I stayed out on the porch, steaming in the frigid air.

I had not talked to my little brother since.

22

"That was the ugliest thing these eyes have ever seen," Big Jim said, snapping me back to the present at St. Mary's Church. "To see my boys saying such awful things to each other...it ripped my heart out."

I looked down at my hands, ashamed of the things I'd said to my little brother. Yes, he had hurt me with his comments, but I was far from innocent in this fight. I could see that now. I certainly was not as innocent as I had convinced myself I was in the years since.

"I didn't mean it to come out so...judgmental," I said. "I was hurt. But I went too far."

"Yes, you did," Big Jim said. "But don't tell me. Tell him."

Even though I knew it was the right thing to do, the thought of apologizing—of telling Andy I was sorry for what I had said—put a knot in my stomach. Why is it so hard to admit when we're wrong?

It wasn't going to be easy, but I knew that at some point I needed to reach out to my brother and try to make amends. He was my brother. And I missed him.

"He misses you too," Big Jim said. He could either read my thoughts supernaturally or he simply knew what I was thinking by the way I was acting, as so many fathers can.

"I let my anger get the best of me that night," I said. "I don't think I've ever been angrier in my adult life. The things he was saying about my life and this town—wouldn't you have been angry at him too?"

"You have to understand that Andy had some big shoes to fill here in Kingstown and, frankly, his heart was never in football the way yours was," Big Jim said. "He had other interests. And for that—no matter how much I assured him otherwise—he always felt like he didn't fit in here."

"I don't remember it that way," I said. "I always remember him getting along with everyone and fitting in great."

"Nobody knows what all is going on in someone else's life. That's why it's so dangerous to judge others."

"Still, can't you agree with me that his career choices and his personal choices have gone against almost everything you taught us?"

"Like all of us, Andy is finding his way; he's doing the best he can," Big Jim said. I could tell he didn't like me asking for his opinion on the matter — almost like he was being asked to gossip about one son with the other.

"Let me ask *you* a question," Big Jim said. "Why do Andy's choices bother you so much? Why can't you just be happy for the success he does have without judging his shortcomings?"

Big Jim always had a way of asking questions that would reveal a person's character.

Why *did* I care so much about Andy's choices? What did *his* choices have to do with my life?

That's when I realized the truth. I didn't want to say it out loud, but I couldn't avoid it any longer.

Big Jim noticed my fidgety reluctance. "Now's the time and this is the place to come clean," Big Jim said.

"I guess — "

" — Don't *guess*; tell me what you know." Another one of Big Jim's favorite lines.

"I don't want to admit this, but there's a part of me that wonders if Andy is right about me," I said.

"Maybe I *was* too scared to leave this place and try something new.

"Earlier I told you that I should have followed a career path more like Andy's—as if it was something I could've easily done if I wanted to. But the truth is, maybe I was scared to go down that path. Looking back, I'm mad at myself for not having the courage to take one of those better jobs when I had the chance. Maybe it keeps me up at night wondering if Andy is right about me and I've let my family down because I was too afraid to push myself and see how far I could've climbed. Maybe I look at Andy's life and think, *that's* what I should've done."

"You really believe that?" Big Jim asked. He wasn't judging. I had no idea if he thought my feelings were right or wrong.

I turned to my dad and said, "With everything that's happening now, I *know* that."

23

"You've got to stop comparing your life to Andy's or anybody else's," Big Jim said. "God places certain passions in each of our hearts and it's our job to follow them. Your interests and passions are unique to you. Your heart was here and you followed it. It's not easy to always follow your heart—as you're finding out now—but it's better than the alternative."

"How do you know?" I asked. "How do you know it's better than the alternative? I *know* I could've been successful at the next level. If I had taken those opportunities I would probably be a millionaire today and I'd still be doing something I love: coaching football."

"I believe you would've been successful as well, but would you have truly been following your heart?"

"You know what, Dad? I don't care anymore. I should've been smarter about my decisions and taken better opportunities when I had the chance. My instincts told me to stay here, but my instincts were wrong!"

"You sure about that?"

"I have no doubt in my mind," I said. "Look at what has happened to me, my family, this school, and this town? I should've gotten out of here when I had the chance. I should've gone after bigger paydays and better opportunities.

"All this follow-your-heart stuff is wrong. Can't you see that now? The end result is missed opportunities and failure."

I could see that my words hurt my father. He rubbed his forehead and said, slowly and quietly, "If that's the way you feel, I can help you."

I looked at Big Jim. "What do you mean?"

His gaze was downward and he looked as though he wished the conversation hadn't come to this. "I don't have the power to save the school or your pension, but I can take you back to one moment in your life and offer you the chance to take a different path. This is an opportunity that most people never get. If you want to go back, relive a moment, and change a major decision, I can give you that opportunity."

"That's impossible," I said.

He looked at me and, with a sarcastic tone, said, "Oh, but it *is* possible for you to be sitting here having a conversation with your old man thirty years after he died?"

I smiled. "Fair point."

I thought about the possibilities. *If I could go back to one moment in my life, what would it be? What would I change?*

The first thing that popped into my head was one of my state championship games. What coach hasn't questioned a call here and a call there? I could change the trajectory of one of those games and *finally* win a state title.

But having a state title wouldn't necessarily change a thing about this particular moment. Sure, there's a ripple effect and maybe a well-timed championship would have somehow triggered a chain of events that would have kept the school alive. But that bet was *way* too risky.

Perhaps I should change the Ricky Walsh decision. It was the decision that had haunted me for years, wondering how his life and mine would've ended up differently if I had given him a pass that day and assured him that I would not abandon him.

Maybe he would've been kinder to himself and to our community in the years that followed. But, after talking with Big Jim about it, I'm not so sure I had made the wrong decision with that one.

Should I go back and erase the spiteful things I said to my brother? Certainly, I wish I could take back some of the things I said. However, that particular moment would change nothing at all about my current situation. I could reach out and apologize to Andy at any time. I didn't need to use this once-in-a-lifetime opportunity to go back and change the entire conversation.

I looked at my dad for help. "*Any* moment?"

"Any moment you want to change, we can change it," Big Jim said. "But it's one moment and one moment only. And remember, every moment in our lives changes everything that follows."

With that in mind, I knew the moment I chose had to occur *after* I married Gina. I couldn't possibly take the chance that I wouldn't end up with her as my wife.

The moment had to be something big — something that would undoubtedly change my life for the better. This was my one chance to re-do everything.

The more I thought about it, the more I realized it had to involve accepting one of the job offers I had turned down. That was the only way to ensure that what was currently happening to me — losing my job, my retirement, my school, and my home — would not be happening.

But which job offer should I have accepted?

Too many times to count, other high school programs from all over the nation had called to see if I would be interested in a vacancy. Some of those offers came from Texas and they included six-figure salaries and the type of facilities most high school coaches can only dream of. I often wondered what my life could've been like coaching in the land of *Friday Night Lights* — the high school football capital of the world.

But would life really be that much different for me in Texas? Would I really be that much happier leaving all my friends and extended family members behind? I'd still be a high school coach, only somewhere else. Would I simply be trading the problems I'm dealing with here for similar problems there? And, unlike some people, I think I'd miss the Midwestern weather — I loved the changing seasons, even the winters.

No, I'm a Midwesterner. If I'm coaching high school football I belong here.

Should I have accepted one of the job offers in Ohio or Pennsylvania? No, what would be the point of going back and doing that? With St. Mary's shutting down, that's exactly what I would be trying to do next season if I simply stayed where I was now.

I needed to step up to the next level. I needed to move upward, not laterally.

A couple dozen times in my past, I had been offered college positions. Often when recruiters would come to town, they'd gauge my interest in a college job. (I knew how it worked—they thought they'd have a better opportunity to land a player they were recruiting if they could also add his high school coach to their staff.) Other times, out of the blue, a college coach would decide I'd be a good fit on his new staff.

Most of the college offers I received were for assistant positions at small colleges. These jobs usually didn't pay too well. However, I had received a few Division 1 job offers. These were from major colleges. They included a significant pay raise *and* a pathway to even bigger paydays. If I worked my way up to a Division 1 coordinator or head-coaching job, it could mean a *seven*-figure salary these days.

Through the years, I had serious offers to join three different Big Ten schools: Michigan State, Nebraska, and Indiana. Kentucky from the SEC also came calling once. I knew the main reason they were offering was because they thought I could help them recruit the state of Ohio. Regardless of why they offered me the job, I know if I had joined one of those staffs I could've been successful. I know I could've moved up the ranks quickly.

But still, there was always one job offer that stood out above all the rest. It was an offer to join the Cincinnati Bengals' staff—a job in the National Football League.

A coaching friend from college had put in a good word for me when a new staff was being assembled in Cincinnati back in 1992. They were looking for some young blood. I interviewed three times and was finally offered an entry-level position. Long hours and low pay to start, but it was an entry into the big-time world of professional football.

At the time, I went home and talked to Gina about

it. She told me she would support whatever I decided, but I could tell she was fearful of what the job might entail and how it might change our lives.

I went to the church that evening and prayed about it. I kept asking God to show me what I should do, to guide me to *follow my heart*.

After a restless night's sleep, I decided to stay in Kingstown. I immediately felt a sense of peace about that decision.

But ever since that day, I've wondered how different my life could've been had I taken the Cincinnati job.

Looking back on my life, turning down that opportunity was the decision I most regretted. I nodded at the realization. *That was it; that was the decision I'd like to go back and change.*

"I think I know what I want to go back and do differently," I said to Big Jim. "I want to go back to 1992 and accept the Bengals' job offer."

"Before you make this decision, you need to understand how this works," Big Jim said. "You'll experience your life as it is *right now* if you had made that decision. You don't get to go back and be twenty-nine again. If you choose to change the past, you're going to wake up tomorrow morning as a fifty-three-year-old wherever life has taken you in the years since you accepted the job. Are you willing to accept that?"

I nodded again, though with some hesitation. "It's a risk, but I'm willing to do it."

Anything would be better than the situation I was currently in. I was certain of that.

"You're sure about this?" my dad asked me. "You're *sure* this is what you want to do with your life."

"I *know* I would've been successful," I said. "And I know I would've been able to provide for my family and my future better. I'm sure. Let's do it."

And with that, Big Jim closed his eyes and slowly nodded. "Good luck to you, son."

24

I woke up to the jarring sound of an alarm clock. I shot up in a panic.

Where was I?

What just happened? Where is Big Jim?

Reality began to settle in.

It was all a dream. A very vivid dream, but a dream nonetheless.

I was in bed, it was dark, and I reached over to turn on my bedside lamp. The lamp felt different than I was used to and I had to fumble around to find the switch.

When the light went on, I found myself in a bedroom, but it wasn't *my* bedroom. The bed was huge and the mattress didn't squeak when I rolled over. This wasn't the cramped master bedroom Gina and I had shared for the last twenty-four years; this place was giant, with high ceilings. The floors were not worn-out hardwood and I didn't feel a cold draft leaking in from the old windows. Instead, there was plush carpeting, a large flat-screen TV on the wall, a sitting area off to the left, and a master bathroom that was twice the size of the *bed*room Gina and I were used to.

I must be in a hotel, I thought to myself. *A very nice hotel.*

How did I get here?

Where is Gina?

I was alone in this luxurious room. I swung my legs over and sat up on the side of the bed. I rubbed my eyes as the memories of last night's conversation with Big Jim came rushing back.

It was a dream, I thought to myself. *It had to be. Big Jim didn't come back and I have a state championship to coach today.*

But, why was I in a hotel? Our team played in the early evening and the school couldn't afford a hotel stay. Our plan was to bus out of Kingstown at 11 a.m. and we'd arrive in Columbus, the home of the state championship, by 1:30 p.m.

As I stepped onto the floor, I felt cold air blowing out of the nearby vents. *Why was the air conditioner on in December?*

The next thing I noticed was...my gut. In one night, I had somehow packed on at least thirty pounds. And my back hurt. I was sore as I leaned back and tried to stretch.

What in the world happened to me?!

I looked over to the far side of the room and noticed a framed family picture sitting on the dresser. I walked over to it, my knees hurting as I moved. The picture was of me, Gina, my oldest son Jimmy, and my oldest daughter Lisa. From the looks of it, the photo was taken about ten years ago, but I didn't remember where. *Why would I bring a family portrait to my hotel room? And why aren't my other two kids, Angie and Micky, in the photo?*

I hobbled to the other side of the room, hampered by my sudden girth. I moved the curtains apart and looked through the blinds to see...sunny weather, a gazebo and sparkling swimming pool down below. Not far in the distance, I saw a large blue body of water. It was the ocean. The last thing I remembered was sitting in St. Mary's Church on a cold December night back in Ohio and now I had been transported to an oceanfront...home, not a hotel.

It was all coming back to me now. The offer Big Jim had made me.

"You're going to wake up tomorrow morning as a

fifty-three-year-old wherever life has taken you in the years since you accepted the job," Big Jim had said.

This wasn't a hotel room. This was my *home*. This was my *oceanfront* home.

Big Jim had come through on his promise. This is where I had ended up. And from the looks of things, I was rich. *Very* rich.

A smile came over my face. I didn't feel excitement as much as I felt…relief.

My money problems, my bankrupted pension, the school, my job, my worries about the championship game…the catastrophes that had been consuming my mind, weighing me down, and stressing me out for the past forty-eight hours were all suddenly wiped away.

I looked up to the high ceiling above me and said, "I knew it! I knew I could make it at the next level! Thank you, Dad. Thank you!"

25

I spent the morning exploring my new home like a kid on Christmas Day wondering what new toys he might find. I was also trying to find out details about my new life.

By 11 a.m., I had learned the following about myself: I was rich, I was excessively-fed, I lived in a *huge* mansion, and (according to my driver's license) I lived in Palm Beach, Florida. What I was still unsure of was what I did for a living and where Gina and Micky were.

In a den that had to be mine, I saw pictures of myself on the wall. One was of me coaching the Bengals. Another one showed me wearing a suit and a Jacksonville Jaguars hat while smiling big. This looked like a picture that had been taken at a press conference. At some point in my past, I had been doing something very important for the Jaguars. Was I the head coach?

If I had been the head coach in Jacksonville, I must not be anymore. The NFL regular season would still be going on and I was way too far away from Jacksonville.

Maybe I coached in Miami now? If so, I'm sure I was supposed to be somewhere by this point in the morning. The excitement of discovering my new life was giving way to panic as I struggled to figure out what it was I did for a living and where I was supposed to go next.

Enough guessing. I fired up the computer and Googled myself. My Wikipedia page came up first.

Apparently, I was the *former* head coach of the Jacksonville Jaguars. I held the position for three years and was fired from the job after the 2012 season. My first season, I shocked the NFL with an improbable playoff run that ended with a 13-5 record. My second season, I went 7-9. Third and final season: 6-10. My head coaching record in the NFL was a forgettable 26-24. But still, I had made it to the top of my profession. At some point, I had been a head coach in the National Football League.

Before Jacksonville, I had spent nearly twenty years bouncing around the league. I had worked my way up quickly in Cincinnati and I was the linebackers coach by the 1994 season, which would have been my third year on the staff. After my stint in Cincinnati, I spent time with the Ravens, the Seahawks, the Bears, the Texans, the Chiefs, the Buccaneers, the Raiders, the 49ers, the Ravens again, the Rams, and the Seahawks again, where I served as the defensive coordinator before being hired by Jacksonville as the head coach.

Wow, I thought to myself. *I really made my way around the league.*

Each stint was short, usually just a year or two long. I wondered how Gina and the kids handled all the moving around. Maybe they loved it, living in so many different cities and experiencing so many different communities. Maybe they found all the moves exciting. I hoped so. Knowing Gina the way I did—she was someone who dearly loved being close to her family and friends in Kingstown—I had trouble picturing her being enthusiastic about all the moves. Hopefully, I was wrong. Hopefully, she loved the changing cities and the prosperity my career had obviously brought our family.

Nobody had updated the Wikipedia page to say what I had been doing in the four years since Jacksonville fired me.

Am I retired? Is that why I'm here in Palm Beach, Florida?

Though I was still anxious to learn what I was doing *now*, seeing the Wikipedia page made me happy. I always knew I had what it took to make it big in coaching. And sure enough, I had worked my way to the pinnacle of my profession—a head coaching job in the NFL is as big as it can get for a football coach. I was proud of myself.

I decided to get out of the house and explore my new neighborhood. In my garage, I discovered I was the owner of a Mercedes-Maybach—"like a private jet for the road," as they say.

I smiled big.

I think I'm going to like this new life of mine.

26

It was a gorgeous day. The sun was shining bright and here I was, a kid from Kingstown, Ohio, driving a car worth about three years of my salary back at St. Mary's High School. I glided down the street, passing by one mega-mansion after another. I didn't want to drive too far and end up forgetting where I lived, so I stopped at one of the first restaurants I saw.

It was decorated like a place Jimmy Buffett would've loved and looked more like it belonged in Key West than in an uber-rich Palm Beach neighborhood. More bar than restaurant, I suppose this place was a way for me and my wealthy neighbors to get a sense of *commoner* life once in a while.

"Afternoon, Coach," the man behind the bar shouted to me as soon as I walked in.

It felt good to be recognized. And to be called, "Coach."

"Afternoon," I said, walking up to the bar. "I've

had a crazy morning," I said to the friendly bartender.

"Yeah, what happened?" he said.

How could I begin to explain?

I shook my head with a big smile and said, "You ever have one of those mornings where you wake up and feel like it's the first day of the rest of your life?"

"Every day," my new friend said. "Want your usual?"

I nodded. "That sounds great." Curious what it was.

My "usual" turned out to be a huge double-cheeseburger and fries. I now realized where this mysterious gut of mine had come from.

During my meal, I didn't get a whole lot of answers about what my occupation was. I didn't want the friendly bartender to think I was nuts by asking too many questions, but I got the impression he wasn't surprised at all to see me at the restaurant on a Saturday afternoon. He asked me what I thought of a few college football games that would be on TV later that day and made some small talk about the Dolphins, but it was the way you'd talk to any fellow fan—not the way you'd talk to someone who might be on the coaching staff.

Twice while I was eating, strangers stopped to ask me, "Are you Coach Callahan?" When I said that I was, one asked me for an autograph and the other asked me to take a picture with her. Both strangers told me they were "big fans" and that they didn't think Jacksonville should have let me go.

Apparently, I was rich *and* famous.

After my large meal, I drove back home. I took my time, enjoying the drive and waving at the neighbors I saw walking. It seemed that every home I passed had a meticulously-kept lawn.

In Kingstown, yards varied greatly in my neighborhood. Big Jim always said that when a man let his yard go, it was a sign that he'd also let his pride go. If that was true, about half my Kingstown neighbors were particularly low on pride.

That wasn't the case in my new neighborhood. Nobody parked their cars in the front yard, nobody let weeds overtake the grass, nobody had old sinks or hubcaps or any other useless piece of junk laying in their yard collecting mud and rust. In my Kingstown neighborhood, those eyesores weren't the norm, but they weren't hard to find either. Here in my new neighborhood, such things were nonexistent.

Everything looked fresh and clean and expensive.

Were some of these estates a bit (okay, a lot) ostentatious? Sure, here and there. But I could deal with that. It was a welcome change from the scenery I was used to.

27

When I got back home (it didn't take long for me to start referring to my newfound mansion as *home*), I headed straight for the den—eager to hop online and find out more about myself. Before I got there, I heard the doorbell ring.

I hustled toward the front door, hoping it was someone trustworthy who could provide me with more vital clues about who I was and what I did.

I opened up the door to find my brother standing on the front porch. He was dressed in bright orange pants, a golf shirt, and a visor.

"Andy," I said with a big smile, "It is so great to see you again!"

So overjoyed to see someone I recognized, I forgot about our past-life rivalry and wrapped my arms around my little brother.

"Wow, John, thank you," he said, a bit jolted by my enthusiasm. "I was worried about you. We missed our tee time. Why didn't you answer your phone? I thought something was wrong."

"I can't tell you how glad I am to see you," I said as I held open the door and motioned for him to come inside.

Andy looked at me cautiously as he walked in. "Are you okay, John?"

"I am now," I said, leading him into the kitchen area. "I need you to clue me in on a few things."

"What do you mean?" Andy asked. "And why didn't you show up at the club? Those tee times aren't cheap, you know, and you really hurt--"

"--Oh, uh, it completely slipped my mind," I said.

"This needs to stop, John. I thought you were doing better. I took time out of my schedule to plan this whole thing today. You can't just no-show like that."

"I'm sorry," I said. "I really just—I haven't been myself this morning."

I sat down at the kitchen counter and Andy helped himself to a bottled water from the fridge.

"Andy, can I ask you something that may sound a little strange?"

"Okay," he said, with hesitation in his voice.

"What *exactly* am I supposed to be doing with my life?"

Andy responded not as though he was surprised by my question, but as though he was tired of me asking it. "We've been through this, haven't we?"

"We've been through what?" I asked, excited for a new clue about my life.

"This—this whole thing," he said, making wide circles with his hands aimed at me, like he was sizing me up.

"What whole thing?"

"Your life," Andy said. "Everything is going to be okay. I told you that. We just need to get you back in the game, back at work, all that."

I looked at him, waiting for more.

"John, don't make me go through it all again," he said. "You've missed the last three weeks of work and you can't take another week off. Your clients are starting to ask where you are."

"My *clients*?" I asked.

Andy squinted his eyes at me. "You're not cracking up on me, are you?"

"I know this sounds really weird, but I think I saw Dad last night."

"Okay, now you're scaring me."

"In a dream—or something like a dream," I said.

"Just humor me for a second, will you? Tell me what my job is right now."

Andy looked at me like I was losing my mind.

"Please," I said. "I need to hear you say it."

"You're the executive vice president at Atlas Capital Management."

"I'm not a coach anymore? I thought I'd always be a coach," I said, more to myself than to Andy.

"Just like you tell them, you're a coach for our clients now."

"*Our* clients?" I said. "We work together?"

"Technically, you work *for* me, but yeah, we work together," Andy said with a grin.

I didn't return the smile.

"C'mon, John, I'm just joking. Yes, we work together. We make a great team."

My mind was racing. "I don't coach football anymore?"

Andy again gave me that 'are-you-feeling-okay?' look. "Not since Jacksonville."

"Oh, right," I said, trying to play off my confusion. If I was going to succeed in this new life, I needed to start getting used to it. I didn't want my brother—who apparently was also my boss—

thinking I was crazy.

"You miss it sometimes, huh?" Andy asked.

"I do." I nodded. "I need a drink."

"Whoa," Andy said, putting his hands up. "I thought we agreed it was time to take a break from the booze."

"We did?"

"Don't play dumb, John. You're lucky you didn't end up in jail after your last bender. You don't need a drink. You need some sunshine and some exercise and some...companionship. This is exactly why we were supposed to be golfing this morning with the girls.

"Now, tell me the truth. Tell me why you didn't show up for golf this morning? I told you on Thursday if this whole thing felt too rushed we could call it off."

I didn't respond. *Girls? What girls? My last bender?* I was getting the sense I was going through something bad in this new life of mine.

Andy must have noticed the suddenly-gloomy look on my face. "Hey, who am I to judge?" he said. "If a drink would make you feel better, I'll have one with you."

"What happened to me?" I asked.

"John, we all go through these things. But we all bounce back. You'll see. When you come back to work on Monday, you'll get back in the swing of things and you'll forget about everything that has gone on these last few months."

I was feeling lightheaded. I had done something bad. Something very bad. But what was it? I rubbed my eyebrows.

"Andy? Where is Gina? And where are my kids? It's Saturday, right? Shouldn't they be here?"

"I knew it!" Andy said. "I knew that's why you didn't show up this morning. I told you, if you weren't ready to date again, we didn't have to do it. I'm just trying to help you get back in the game."

"Date?" I asked.

"Don't play dumb," Andy said. "You really hurt Samantha's feelings. She thinks you stood her up this morning.

"Samantha? Wait…slow down, where is Gina?"

Andy blinked his eyes slowly and exhaled. He walked over to me, through his arm over my back, and squeezed my shoulder. "We've been through this, John, it's time to accept what happened. It's time to move on. This isn't healthy."

28

In a delicate game of me trying to not sound *too* crazy while obtaining as much information as I could about my new life, I spent the next hour sitting in the hot sun with Andy out by the pool.

I found out that Gina and I had officially separated two years ago, but that she, Jimmy, and Lisa had moved back to Ohio six years ago. They knew they wouldn't see me much if I was the head coach in Jacksonville, so Gina figured it would be best to live near family back home. According to Andy, I didn't try to convince her otherwise.

Just over a year ago, our divorce was finalized. This sent me on a destructive path. I started drinking heavily. About a month ago, on the anniversary of our divorce, I apparently had some sort of booze-induced meltdown. Andy gave me a few weeks off from work to "clear my head." I had been meeting with a therapist regularly for the past several weeks.

The reason for the separation and divorce? I had been unfaithful.

When Andy told me that, I refused to believe it. I couldn't imagine myself doing such a thing.

"John, there's no use denying it now," Andy said. "It's me you're talking to. I know you regret what you did—you always saw yourself as a Boy Scout growing up—but you said it yourself, you and Gina were over long before you ever met what's-her-name. What *was* her name?"

I didn't respond and Andy didn't wait for an answer.

"You said you were all-but-separated before you even took the Jacksonville job," Andy said. "That was, what, seven years ago?"

"How could I have done this?" I said, again talking to myself more than I was talking to Andy.

"You've got to stop beating yourself up," Andy said. "Yes, you made a mistake. Yes, you should have waited until you were separated before you started seeing other women, but what's done is done. We all make mistakes. Lord knows I have."

As if all this wasn't enough, I found out that my two youngest kids, Angie and Micky, didn't even *exist*. They had never been born. My busy career had taken precedent over having more kids.

On top of that, Andy informed me that a competing company had recently filed a multimillion-dollar lawsuit against me personally — it alleged that I had fraudulently stolen some of their top clients. Andy assured me this was just part of the job, that I needed to have thick skin to handle the stress, and that our company was juggling multiple such lawsuits.

What have I done with my life?

Andy tried to cheer me up the only way Andy knew how.

"You make more money in a year than most people make in a lifetime," he said. "You live in a home most people can only dream of. You're great at your job and people like and respect you. You'll meet someone else, trust me on that one.

"I hate to see you beating yourself up like this. It's unhealthy. What would Dad say if he saw you wallowing in this kind of self-pity?"

"He would say I should've followed my heart and done the right thing," I said. "He would say I should have put my faith and my family above my career."

"No, he'd say this world is a tough place and a man's got to do what a man's got to do," Andy said.

"He'd say you gave your all to coaching and when Jacksonville fired you, you refused to stay down. You picked yourself up, you took control of your life and you decided to try something new. And guess what? You now make twice as much working with me than you did as a head coach in the NFL! Things turned out better for you than you ever could have imagined."

"How can you say that?" I asked. "How can you say things turned out *better* for me?"

"Look around you," Andy said. "You've made it big. You don't have to worry about money or job security. You're famous and successful. You've lived life to the fullest. Look at how far you've come!

"Have you hit a rough patch? Sure, but it's nothing you can't overcome. I've told you a thousand times not to worry about the lawsuit; they don't have a case and you can't let yourself get stressed out about it.

"As for the divorce, lots of guys go through them. I've been through two already! It sucks, but it's a part of life. You'll get back in the game. Trust me, it gets better.

"And you should be happy you ended up as well

as you did in this whole deal. Gina could've gone after all your assets. She could've buried you. Let's be honest, if you're going to go through hard times, it's better to be rich and living large here in Palm Beach than it is to be broke and living in a dead-end place like Kingstown, which is where she is now. Am I right?"

"I'm not so sure," I said.

Andy furrowed his eyebrows. "You *can't* be serious."

"I am," I said. "I'm fifty-three years old and what do I have to show for my life?"

Andy huffed. "Look around you, look at everything--"

"--Yes, yes, I know, I've made lots of money, I have a huge house, and I drive expensive cars. But is this all life is about? Do I have a family that loves me? Do I have a job I love?"

"Hey, I know the job is a grind and it can feel like we're selling our souls sometimes, but if it was easy everybody would do it. This is why we make the big bucks. Because we're willing to do what others aren't."

"I don't care about the money!" I shouted.

Andy shook his head, as though he was offended by my declaration. "I guess I'll have to remember that the next time we discuss your salary and commission structure."

"My point is…" I paused, unsure exactly what to say next.

"Yes?" Andy said. "What *is* your point in all this?"

"My point is…am I happy? Are *you* happy?"

"I'm happy when I see my account balance every morning."

"Don't do that," I said. "Don't make it all about the money. Yes, we all want to be rich, but you and I both know there are more important things in life. Things like Dad always told us. Things like faith, family, and community. Are you happy? Are you truly happy?"

Andy looked away, silent for a moment.

"Could I be happier?" he asked. "Sure, who couldn't be?"

"No," I said. "Don't blow me off. Look at us. Yes, we're rich. Yes, we're comfortable. Yes, we're well-known, we're well-respected, we're successful, and we're apparently powerful. But, are either of us happy?"

"We should be," Andy said. "Look at everything we've accomplished. Do you know how many people in this world wish they were us? Do you know how many people are jealous of you and me?"

"Are you happy?" I asked again.

Andy looked up at the sky and exhaled. "I get depressed when I think about happiness. That's pretty messed up, isn't it?"

"Yes, it is."

"What do you want me to say, John? That I'm miserable and lonely? That I wake up in the night sometimes and ask myself, 'Is this all there is?' What would saying such things accomplish?"

"It would force you to examine your life. It would force you to consider other options."

"What other options?" Andy asked.

"This isn't what I was supposed to do with my life," I said. "And it sounds like you feel the same way."

"Even if that was true, it's too late now."

"It's never too late."

"You want to just throw everything away—the company I've built from the ground up and that you helped grow? What for? So I can *find myself* and *follow my bliss*? Get serious, big brother. You're having a midlife crisis. Maybe we both are. But we're in it this far and there's no going back now. I've invested too much time, energy, and money to get to where I am. We both have."

"You can't cling to a mistake just because you spent a lot of time making it," I said.

Andy had no response.

29

In a very short period of time, I went from loving my new life to despising all that I had become.

After Andy left, I spent the rest of the day piecing together what I could about how I'd gotten to where I was. The biggest help was a few half-filled journals I found locked in my desk drawer. There weren't daily entries—often weeks or even months would pass between entries—but there was enough to clue me in on the major events that had happened in my life.

I learned that the years of bouncing around from job to job had been very tough on Gina and the kids. She wanted to stay near family and friends in Ohio. She wanted stability. Big arguments had preceded each new move. We lived in separate cities during *four* of my coaching stops. Living across the country from each other like that, it's no wonder we grew apart.

I also learned that my relationship with my kids was...*strained*—to put it kindly.

When I went through text messages on my phone, I discovered that I spent a lot of time virtually begging both Jimmy and Lisa to come spend time with me here in Florida. These invitations were either ignored or declined multiple times.

"Dad, I have a life of my own now," Lisa had texted me. "You can't expect the world to stop for everyone else because Jacksonville fired you and you finally have some time on your hands. I needed you when I was growing up. I don't need you now."

Ouch. I could not imagine my sweet daughter — the Lisa I knew — saying something so cruel to me.

Nor could I imagine myself texting the response I did: "You don't need me? Does that mean you don't need all those checks I send to you and your brother?"

My heart sank. I had become a petty, dead-beat father.

How could this happen? How could my personality and my values have changed so much? All because of one little decision almost twenty years ago?

This didn't make sense. Where I was and what I did may have changed, but how did *who* I was change so much?

Several times, I openly called for Big Jim to return to me. I wanted some answers. I wanted to know if my decision was irreversible. I had specifically chosen to change a moment in time *after* Gina and I were married so that I wouldn't risk screwing that up. Life without Gina and my kids — all *four* of my kids — was not supposed to be part of this deal!

"This isn't fair!" I shouted to the tall ceiling in my silent living room as the day turned to dusk. "I want to go back to who I was before. At least let me change some other decisions. There must be a way! Why did one single career decision have to change *everything* about my life? Why not let me go back and change other decisions along the way? Give me a chance to keep my family together. Dad, can you hear me? This isn't fair. This wasn't part of the deal!"

Big Jim never responded.

I started to wonder if I was crazy. Was this all one horrible nightmare? An awful hallucination? Or, was my previous life in Kingstown the hallucination?

An odd thing began to happen when the evening arrived. I started to slowly *remember* moments that I never *experienced* first-hand. These were moments that would have happened prior to my encounter with Big Jim in the church and after my decision to take the Cincinnati job. My new life was becoming my actual life.

I saw past moments of me yelling at Gina — her in tears while I accused her of trying to sabotage my career.

One particular memory saw me telling Gina we were broke. "I promise to never let this happen again," I said.

"I don't care about the money," Gina said. "I just want you to be happy. I want *us* to be happy. I want to be a family again."

Another memory showed me talking with another woman, a woman I'd never seen before this memory popped into my head. I told her, "My wife doesn't even live here. She abandoned me. She doesn't like all the pressure that comes with this job."

"Sounds like you need someone who appreciates you," the woman said.

I shook my head, trying to physically shake out the memory.

How could I be so selfish? I thought to myself.

I decided I had to call Gina. I had to talk to my

wife, my best friend. I couldn't bear the thought of not having her in my life. I had to make things right.

Her number was on my cell phone. I dialed it and held my breath.

30

"Gina, I'm so glad you answered!" I said as soon as I heard her voice.

"John, have you been drinking again?" she said in a tone that sounded tired—not physically tired, but tired of having this conversation.

"No, not a drop, I promise. I just had to talk to you. I had to tell you something."

"What is it?" she said.

"I want you to know that all the terrible things I did, that wasn't me. It wasn't the real me. I don't know who it was, but it wasn't me. I'm so sorry I put you and the kids through all this. I don't know how to explain it, but it wasn't me. You've got to believe me! I would never do that to you. You've *got* to believe me!"

She sighed. "Oh, then who was it?"

How was I supposed to respond?

When I couldn't think of a way to answer her question, I simply told her the truth. "I think I'm losing my mind."

"John, you need help," Gina said. "I thought you were seeing a psychiatrist."

"I know how this sounds, but something happened to me last night. It's like my whole world got turned upside down. Yesterday, you were my wife and we had a great family in Kingstown. Things weren't perfect, but we were together. We were a family. And then today, I wake up and discover I'm a dirt-bag husband and a dead-beat father."

"Life happens fast, doesn't it?" Gina said.

"That's not what I mean." I said. "That's not what I'm trying to say."

I was frustrated. There was so much I wanted to explain but it would all sound ridiculous if I said it out loud.

"What *are* you trying to say?" Gina asked.

"I guess I'm saying…will you forgive me?"

"I already told you I've forgiven you, several times."

"You did?"

"I've moved on with my life and you need to move on with yours," Gina said.

"Can you give me another chance?" I asked. "Can you *please* let me prove to you that I'm not who you think I am? I'm not that guy you've known for the last…"

I paused, realizing how pathetic this must sound.

"For the last twenty years?" Gina asked.

"I know it sounds crazy," I said. "But if you just give me the chance to prove it, I *promise* you won't be sorry."

After a long moment of silence, Gina said, "John, you have to stop calling. I wish you the best, I really do, but you have to move on with your life."

And with that, she hung up.

31

I couldn't believe this was happening. My wife — or, ex-wife — had just hung up on me. My kids — the two that I had — wouldn't talk to me. My life in coaching — the career I loved — was over.

I was rich, famous, and successful, both as a coach and now as some sort of financial guy, but I couldn't live like this. If Big Jim wouldn't come back to me and answer my questions, I was going to have to find him — in the only place I knew he might be.

I hopped in my Mercedes and drove north. I drove for four or five hours until I had to find a hotel and get some sleep. As soon as I woke up the next morning and realized this nightmare was still happening, I got back in the car and continued on my way. I drove ten-straight hours before calling it a day.

The next morning — this would have been Monday — I arrived in Kingstown.

It was a cloudy gray day and the town looked...different. It was less welcoming, less charming. It looked more beat up. It looked grimier, like it needed a good scrub. There weren't any Christmas lights outlining the Main Street buildings and there were fewer cars parked in front of Kingstown's downtown shops. Some of the buildings I personally had helped paint several years ago—in my past life—hadn't been touched up at all. There were more abandoned shops than I remembered. Patti's Place, my sister's bar and restaurant, didn't exist. Bob's Diner still had a FOR SALE sign in the window, but it looked like the place had been closed for years.

How had this happened? How had the town fallen so far downhill since I had left? I wasn't arrogant enough to believe that my presence as the football coach at St. Mary's High School made that big of a difference.

Something else must have caused the decline.

Before heading to the school and church, I drove to the Victory Sportswear headquarters and saw, just as I feared, an abandoned building with broken windows and KEEP OUT, NO TRESPASSING signs posted all over the property. Yet another shuddered factory in Kingstown, Ohio.

I drove down Oak Street and stopped in front of my home — or, the house that had been my home in a previous life. The house was run down, desperately in need of a paint job. The yard was now one of those that lacked pride with overgrown weeds and rusty junk strewn all over it. The front porch I had spent so many nights sitting on visiting with family and friends was half-gone, the wood rotted through and never replaced.

Tears welled up in my eyes. What was once a warm, cozy, welcoming home now looked *dangerous*.

I drove two blocks further to the St. Mary's campus. The first thing I noticed was the grotto. Normally a bright, welcoming sight with most of the candles within it lit up, I saw just two candles flickering. If each candle represented somebody's hopeful prayer, there clearly wasn't much hope left around here.

As I pulled into the St. Mary's Church parking lot, I noticed that while the elementary school looked active — with child-made construction paper cutouts in the windows and typical school messages out front — the high school looked abandoned. There was no sign of activity and the parking lot was empty except for two cars that looked like they hadn't been moved in months, maybe years.

I walked up the steps of St. Mary's Church and silently prayed that Big Jim would be waiting for me inside.

32

There he was, sitting in the second pew from the front, just as I had last seen him. The man who had given me a once-in-a-lifetime opportunity, which ended up ruining my life.

"I thought you'd be showing up here sooner or later," my dad said without turning around.

"You tricked me," I said.

That got him to turn my way. "How so?"

I stormed down the aisle and stopped when I got to the front of the church. I stood over my father.

"You said I could change a moment in my life," I said. "I knew that would change where I lived and what I did, but you didn't tell me it would change *who* I was. I wanted an opportunity to provide a better life for my family, not to *lose* my family."

Big Jim scooted down the pew and motioned for me to have a seat next to him.

"Every decision we make in our lives has a ripple effect," he said. "Every decision affects your faith, your family, your work, your health, and your community. I've been telling you this your whole life. Why are you surprised to see it happen now?"

I sat down next to Big Jim, still upset at him. I felt duped.

"What happened to me would *not* have happened to me," I said. "Something went wrong. That wasn't me. I would never, ever be unfaithful to Gina. I would *never* abandon my family like that. I would never choose money and career status over my faith and my family. That wasn't me."

"It was you," Big Jim said. "You got your priorities mixed up and they stayed mixed up. You put fortune and fame above everything else. When you got offered the Cincinnati job, you thought about it long and hard. You talked about it with Gina and you knew she didn't want you to take it."

"How was I supposed to know that? She said she would support whatever decision I made."

Big Jim looked me in the eye. "Don't play dumb. You knew."

I looked down. He was right.

"You knew, in your heart, that life in the NFL—despite being a great opportunity—wasn't the right path for you," Big Jim said. "But, you took it anyway.

"And, you had great success, you became a famous coach, and you made a ton of money along the way.

"But, those things—fortune and fame—became your priorities. You placed them above your faith, your family, your health, and your community. Not all at once, mind you, but through the years the fame and fortune became more and more important to you. They eventually became your *top* priorities; you put them above everything else."

"But my faith should've kept me from doing what I did to Gina," I said. "I was taught right from wrong. I would not have abandoned my faith and my morals."

"You didn't abandon your faith all at once," Big Jim said. "You let it slowly slip away. At St. Mary's High School you taught Religion class. Every day on your way home, you stopped at the grotto to pray. Practicing your faith was an everyday part of your life. But in your new life, that changed. It became less and less a part of your daily routine. Soon, you barely thought about it at all.

"Everything you did was focused on your work and getting ahead. And it wasn't even work you enjoyed. There were many times throughout your life where you recognized this. You questioned whether you were on the right path. You missed working with young adults and shaping their lives as a high school teacher and coach. You missed your friends and family back in Kingstown. You thought about walking away from the high-stress, bottom-line world of the NFL.

"Several times, Gina tried to convince you to go back to a high school job where the two of you could have a more stable lifestyle, where you could become part of a closer community, and where you could make a more significant difference in the lives of young people. But when push came to shove, you couldn't walk away from the money you were making and the attention you were receiving as a coach in the pros.

"Even after you lost your job in the NFL, you went looking for a new career that would give you even more power, wealth, and prestige. You went into finance after coaching because you couldn't stand the idea of making less money. Again, you chose fame and fortune over what your heart was telling you to do.

"It became a vicious cycle. You became a slave to work that you didn't enjoy. By the end of your coaching career, you were burned out. Your passion for the game had dwindled. You didn't believe you were making a positive difference in people's lives the way you did at St. Mary's. Going to work every morning became a grind for you.

"Working in finance was even worse, but you were addicted to the money and the prestige that came with the big house and the fancy cars. That's what drove you—not work that you were passionate about.

"Some people love working in the NFL. Some people have a true passion for the world of finance. But that wasn't you, that wasn't your passion. You weren't being true to yourself in those careers. It was all about what those careers could give you, not what you could give them.

"Through the years, you left your faith behind, your health deteriorated, and you never got involved with your community as you hopped around from place to place. And, well, you already know what it did to your family."

"But all from one decision?" I said. "How could

that be?"

"You got your priorities mixed up and you stopped listening to your heart. When you lose track of the things that are most important, life tends to get messy. *Everything* changes. Some of those changes may seem good at first-glance, but they end up bad in the long run.

"Money, power, fame—those things aren't *bad* in and of themselves and it's fine if they're part of your goals. But, if you make those things your *top* priorities, you'll never find true happiness. You'll never find peace of mind."

"Why can't I have both?" I asked. "Why not the best of both worlds? Money, job security, *and* my family, my faith, and my health?"

"Who says you can't have both?" Big Jim asked.

"Life does," I said. "Look at how it all ended up me for me here in Kingstown."

"Look at how it ended up for you in Palm Beach. Which version of you was more successful?"

I thought about this for a moment and said, "But some people get both. Some people make tons of money and also have a strong family and faith life. Why can't that be me?"

"There you go again, comparing your life to others," Big Jim said. "First off, everyone has problems. No matter how it may look on the outside, nobody *has it all*. Everyone has worries and challenges they're dealing with. You've got to stop comparing yourself to others. You've got to be content with following *your* path, not comparing it to somebody else's."

"I see your point, but that doesn't answer my question," I said. "I'm not asking to be the richest guy in town. I just want to know why things couldn't have ended up better for me here in Kingstown."

Big Jim leaned back slowly and smiled. "I have what you'd call a more *eternal* perspective these days. And one thing I've come to see is that every one of us is born for a path that is unique to us. God chose you before the world was created, before there were stars in the sky, and before there was any such thing as the universe. Think about that for a second. He chose you for a very specific journey. He had a plan for your life. This unique plan is your purpose and it affects many people and places—in ways you can't begin to see. Your purpose is yours and yours alone. You need to follow *your* path, not somebody else's.

"You're here for a reason and God has a plan for your life," Big Jim continued. "You have to trust in that plan. Everybody's path is different. Each individual's heart calls him in a different direction. And every path requires sacrifices that are unique to it. There will always be sacrifices that must be made for the things that are most important to you. That's why you have to keep your priorities straight at all times.

"You have to trust God's plan for your life."

"That's easier said than done," I said. "How can I trust God's plan if I'm unsure what that plan is? I never would have accepted the Cincinnati job if I knew it would result in me sacrificing all the things that were so important to me. How are we supposed to be sure we're following God's plan for our lives?"

"When you follow your heart, you'll feel an inner peace," Big Jim said. "Fame and fortune can't bring you that peace. Those things might find you, but they won't bring you peace if that's all you have. Only by following your heart and keeping your priorities straight will you find that inner peace. When you have that peace inside—when you feel it deep in your soul—you'll know you're following your purpose, God's plan for you.

"Don't misunderstand me. Having inner peace doesn't mean there won't be challenges. It doesn't mean there won't be times of struggle and worry about what the future holds. Having inner peace doesn't mean living a carefree life where everything always goes your way. There will be pain and there will be disappointment, but deep down you'll know in your heart that you're on the right path and that you can overcome whatever challenges might come your way."

"But why does everything have to be *so* hard here in Kingstown?" I asked again. I *needed* an answer. "If this was God's plan for my life, if my purpose was here at St. Mary's, why did I have to lose my job, my team, my hometown, and my pension? Why does God have to make it *so hard*?"

"I can't answer that," Big Jim said. "I don't know why things happen the way they do and I don't know what the future will bring you or this town. What I do know is that things tend to work out as long as you keep your priorities straight and follow your heart.

"Like I've always taught you, you can't control all

the events that happen in your life, but you can control how you *respond* to those events. As long as you respond to adversity by keeping your priorities in order and living your unique purpose, you can trust that everything will work out in the end.

"And remember, there is a bigger plan than you can see. Your path is unique to you and it affects many other people. You were made for a greater purpose here, in Kingstown, than you may realize. The lives you were supposed to affect—the impact you were supposed to have on your family, your students, your friends, and this community—it's all part of a bigger plan than you can see.

"Look at how this town has changed since you left it. You must have made a bigger impact than you realize.

"Your life here in Kingstown was a special part of your unique journey. And maybe God has decided that chapter of your journey is over. Maybe you have accomplished all that you were called to accomplish here in this community and God is leading you somewhere else.

"I don't know what the future holds for you. What I do know is that when you don't follow your heart and live your unique purpose, you turn your back on a much greater plan—God's plan for your life. And when you do that, things don't turn out so well…for you or the other people in your life.

"No matter what obstacles and unforeseen challenges come your way, if you keep your priorities straight and if you always follow your heart, I promise you it will be better than the alternative. In the long run, things will end up alright for those who follow their hearts. Take comfort in that. Have peace knowing that."

33

"I just wish it didn't have to end up so miserably," I said to Big Jim.

"Which path made you miserable?" my dad asked. "The one where you were famous, wealthy, and powerful—but without a family? Or, the one where you were here, in Kingstown, at St. Mary's High School, living with Gina?"

"Obviously, I'd rather be here, with my family. But both scenarios ended badly in their own ways."

"Neither scenario *has* ended," Big Jim said. "Neither journey has reached the end. Anyone can change their path at any moment. If you haven't been following your heart and living your purpose, the best time to start is *now*!

"Regardless of which path you choose to stay on, you create your tomorrow by what you do today."

"You mean I can choose to go back and keep the life I had here in Kingstown?" I asked, suddenly excited about the option.

"Yes, you can. If you choose, you can walk out

these doors and your life will be just as it was when you walked in here on Friday night.

"Or, you can continue on this alternative path. You can walk out of here, get back into your fancy car, try to reconnect with Gina, and change your life going forward.

"You wanted to see what your life would've been like and you've seen it. Now, you get to choose which path you want to continue on.

"Just remember that nobody knows what tomorrow brings. I certainly don't. Neither path is easy. If you choose to go back to the way things were, you'll still be facing a tough situation with the school closing, your job and pension gone, and the biggest game of your coaching career on Saturday."

"I understand," I said. "And it's a no-brainer. I want Gina and my kids back. I want my family back. I want my team back for one last game. And I want my community back…even if I have to leave it.

"At least I'll be able to look myself in the mirror and be proud of who I am."

I then saw something I had never seen before. I saw a tear run down my father's cheek.

"I'm proud of you, son. So proud."

Suddenly, I felt peace rush over me. No matter what tomorrow might bring, I knew this was where I belonged. I didn't know where I'd be next year and I didn't know what would happen to Kingstown and the community I loved in the future, but I did know that whatever happened next, I would be better off in this scenario. I would be better off following my heart.

Here, I would be the person I was meant to be.

"Thank you," I said to Big Jim. "Thank you for showing me what I could've been. Thank you for making me appreciate what I have."

He nodded. "You've been given a special gift. Most people spend their whole lives wondering what could've been had they chosen something different. You got to see it. You've been given a whole new appreciation for your life, regardless of the hardships that may be coming your way. Don't waste this gift."

"I won't," I said.

I then turned to my dad and said, "Can I ask you for one more favor?"

Big Jim eyed me suspiciously and waited for my request.

"Can you help me out tomorrow, in the state

championship?" I asked. "I know there are greater things at stake for this community, but if I can leave this program the way I knew it, as the best in the state, it will be a legacy that nobody ever forgets. If we win tomorrow, St. Mary's High will always be known as the only program that *finished* on top. And I will no longer be known as the coach who couldn't win the big one."

"I'll see what I can do," Big Jim said with a smile. "You give it everything you have tomorrow and I have a feeling it'll turn out well for you."

"I will, and thank you."

"I have a favor to ask of you as well."

"Anything," I said.

"When you go home tonight, call your brother. You got to walk in his shoes for a little while and you saw that his life isn't as rosy as you assumed. You also saw how easy it was for you yourself to end up on the path he's currently living. He needs you."

I nodded. "I need him too."

34

Big Jim and I said our goodbyes shortly thereafter. I told my dad how much I missed him and loved him and he said the same. He promised to be watching over me in what would be the last game of my career at St. Mary's High School.

When I walked out of the church, it was as though the previous sixty hours or so had never happened. It was nighttime, the lights were on at the high school, the grotto's candles were bright and beautiful, my excessive gut had vanished, and there was no Mercedes-Maybach parked out front.

The only change I noticed since first walking into the church Friday night was that the wind had picked up and grown colder. Snow was on the way. You could feel it.

For a moment, I felt like George Bailey in *It's a Wonderful Life*. I had the urge to joyfully run through the Kingstown streets yelling "Merry Christmas" to everyone I saw.

I laughed off the urge and stopped at the grotto to

light one more candle.

When I got home, I gave Gina the longest hug and kiss I'd ever given her. I had never been so glad to see her.

"We're going to be alright," I said. "No matter what happens, as long as you and I are together, everything's going to be just fine."

"I know that," Gina said. "I always have and I always will."

Before I went to bed, I called Andy.

He didn't answer, so I left a message: "Andy, this is John. I know this is way out of the blue, but it's long overdue. Something happened to me tonight that finally made me realize what a jerk I was to you the last time we talked. I'm sorry for the things I said to you. Please accept my apology and know that I care about you. You're my brother and I love you. I respect you, I miss you, and I hope that we can reconnect soon. Call me when you get this, no matter how late. Happy belated Thanksgiving and an early Merry Christmas to you, Andy — I hope all is going well."

But Andy didn't call me back.

35

When I woke up Saturday morning, the snow was falling and the wind was howling. I couldn't help but wonder if this weather was a gift from Big Jim. Our team would be facing the No. 1-ranked Glendale Park Trojans in the state championship game. They ran the Air Raid spread offense and liked to throw the ball all over the field. At St. Mary's, we ran a conservative, run-heavy, triple-option offense. Adverse weather conditions like this usually favored our style of play.

Before a game, some coaches are at their most relaxed state. All the work and preparation has been done. There's a certain comfort that comes from knowing you've done everything you can, your team is as prepared as they can be, and there's nothing else you can do. My dad, Big Jim, was like that. He was always cheerful and confident on game day.

Other coaches tend to be a nervous wreck on game day. They get as anxious as some of their players. Their stomachs turn as the hours tick away prior to kickoff. I was usually that type of coach.

But today was different.

After everything that had happened the night (or days) before, I was content. I was grateful for who I was, where I was, and the opportunity in front of me.

As we rode in the bus to Columbus, I wasn't nervous about our opponent. I wasn't thinking about what the future might hold for St. Mary's High School or for me and my family. I wasn't my normal anxious and agitated self on game day. I was grateful. I was confident. I was at peace.

The players and coaches could sense this. The fact that I kept repeating the phrase, "It's gonna' be a great day," surely helped lighten the tension that often accompanied a pregame bus ride.

Something inside of me just knew that things were going to go our way today. Perhaps because I had an angel on my shoulder...and that angel was named Big Jim Callahan, the greatest coach in the history of St. Mary's High School football.

36

The 2016 Ohio high school football state championship games were all played at Ohio Stadium, home of the Ohio State Buckeyes. It was a great opportunity for our players to experience big-time college football facilities. I told the team to enjoy it, to embrace the moment. I didn't want them so nervous about the game that they failed to take in what would be a once-in-a-lifetime opportunity for almost everyone on the team.

Our game, the Division VII championship, had a 5 p.m. scheduled kickoff. The snow had fallen on and off all afternoon and the wind gusts were consistently strong. By the time we took the field for warmups, the temperature was in the twenties and an inch of snow was sitting on the field. We could not have asked for a better scenario to help us ground Glendale Park's pass-happy offense.

After warmups, we went back to the locker room for some final words before taking the field. It was at this moment that I realized I was about to give my *last* pregame speech as the head football coach at St. Mary's High School. The emotion hit me and I tried my best to keep it together. I didn't want our players thinking I was losing it before the game.

"Men, you're about to take the field for the final time," I said to the team. "No matter what happens out there tonight, I want you to know that I'm proud of everything you've done to get to this point. You've accomplished what very few teams are able to accomplish. Every kid who has ever picked up a football has dreamed about running through that tunnel and playing for a championship. But only an elite few ever get to do it. You are one of the elite few. Make the most of this opportunity."

Some of our players shouted out, a few clapped.

"I know this moment feels big," I continued. "We all know there's a lot more at stake than a championship trophy. You men will represent this proud football program for the last time ever. When people remember St. Mary's High School, they're going to always remember what they see tonight. *You* will be the last faces of St. Mary's High. *You* will be what people remember.

"I bring up this fact not to add to the pressure you

may be feeling, but to remind you that you're part of something very special. You're the final chapter in one of Ohio high school football's greatest stories. And I can't think of a better group of young men to represent St. Mary's for the final time than each of you."

A few more claps. "Panther pride, baby," I heard our defensive captain shout.

"This program was built on the culture Big Jim built," I said. "As you've heard a million times, that culture consists of faith, family, courage and character. Everything you've done up to this point has been done with faith, courage, and character. And we've done it as a family. You've done everything we've asked of you with a positive attitude and a relentless work ethic. I could not be prouder of this group than I am right now. You are the epitome of what it means to be a St. Mary's Panther and I want you to always take pride in that."

I saw some nods and some nervous twitching. The energy was building in this locker room. The players needed to be unleashed. But I wasn't done yet.

"It has always meant something special to be a St. Mary's Panther. It meant you were part of something bigger than yourself. You were part of a tradition unlike any other. You were part of a tight community. You were part of a *family* — a family that loves you. Nothing can ever take that away from you.

"I don't have to tell you that life isn't always fair. A lot of things happen that you have no control over. It happens in football and, as you're all seeing this week, it happens in life. But there is nothing to fear. I promise you that. If you march forward in faith, if you attack the day with courage, if you do things with character, and if you always put your family first; you *will* be successful. *Nothing* can stop you."

More claps, more shouts; the noise and energy was rising.

"You can't control everything. But you *can* control the most important things. You can control your effort and your attitude. They can take away your school, they can take away your team, and they may even be able to take away your hometown; but they can't take your pride, your effort, or your attitude."

"No, they can't!" I heard one of our players shout.

"They can't take away your faith."

"No, they can't!" I heard a handful of players

shout in unison.

"They can't take away your courage." My voice was rising.

"No, they can't!" the entire team shouted.

"They can't take away your character." Louder still.

"No, they can't!" They all shouted again.

"And they can't take away *your family*!" I shouted in a booming voice that I could've sworn sounded exactly like Big Jim's.

"No, they can't!" the entire team roared.

"Tonight, as a family, for one last time, as brothers in arms, we will prove that nothing—*NOTHING*—can ever tear *this family* apart!"

A deafening roar overwhelmed me as the players shouted, pounded on each other's pads, and finally rushed through the locker-room door.

We took the field with an emotional high I had never before experienced as a coach or as a player.

This was going to be a special night.

37

The Glendale Park Trojans had been the most dominant Division VII program in the state over the last decade. Their thirty-nine-year-old coach was already looking for his fourth state title in the last seven years. As everyone in the stadium knew, I was still looking for my *first* state title.

The Trojans were also notorious trash-talkers. And that started with their head coach, Lance Morgan. In an interview on Friday, he was asked what it would mean to be the opponent in our school's final game.

"Honestly, I feel kind of bad about it," the brash young coach said. "I hate to be the one to rain on their parade and I know how much it would mean to their coach to finally win a championship ring after all his years of trying. I'm sure it seems unfair that I've been winning so many and I'm only, like, half his age. But, it is what it is. We can't just give state titles to whoever wants one. They have to be earned."

When asked to respond to his comments, I declined. I planned on letting our performance do the talking.

As I walked onto the field, I noticed the Glendale Park fans had hung a huge banner behind their team's bench. It said: BEAT THE DINOSAURS. It was a clear reference to the fact that we were has-beens in their eyes—a soon-to-be-extinct program clutching to the past.

I chuckled at the sign. There was some truth to it. As teams, we were polar opposites. They had a young, cocky coach who ran a fast-paced, pass-first modern offense. We ran an old-fashioned control-the-clock, run-first offense. Their team liked to talk, our team liked to keep quiet and let our actions do the talking. It was a classic battle of new school versus old school.

Glendale Park won the coin toss and elected to receive the ball. They drove right down the field as if the snow and wind had no effect whatsoever.

After a first-down completion near our sidelines, the receiver who caught the ball turned to us and said, "No wonder their shutting down your school. You all are stuck in the past. Nobody wants you around anymore. Nobody."

Like all trash talk is intended to do, his words were meant to antagonize our players, get them out of their game, and cause them to make mistakes. I have to admit, his words stung even me. They encapsulated exactly what a lot of us were feeling.

The Trojans used a hurry-up tempo and short passes to march down to our 12-yard line with no problem.

Dad, I could use a hand right about now, I silently said to myself.

Their quarterback was lined up in the shotgun and when the center snapped the ball, a sudden gust of wind sent it higher than the quarterback expected. We had called a blitz and our linebacker, my son, Micky Callahan, rushed into the backfield. As the quarterback bobbled the high snap and tried to regain control of the football, Micky hit him so hard you could hear it up in the press box, I was later told. The ball went flying backwards and players from both teams dove for it. When the refs unpiled the bodies, it was our ball at the 20-yard line.

The fans on our side of the stadium, a good five thousand strong, let out a roar.

Micky ran back to the sidelines yelling with excitement, "They can't tear us apart! They can't tear this family apart!"

My eyes were misty with pride.

"No, they can't," I said quietly while giving a nod to the night sky and envisioning Big Jim watching over us.

We responded by doing what we do best, marching down the field with one run after another and chewing up the clock. We scored on an 8-yard option pitch to take a 7-0 lead with a little over three minutes left in the first quarter.

Glendale Park wanted to play in games where their offense could march down the field multiple times per quarter in break-neck speed. They hated our style of play.

Welcome to old-school football, I thought to myself. *You have no idea what you're going up against tonight.*

38

We took a 14-0 lead into halftime. It was the first time all season that Glendale Park had been held scoreless for a half. The weather had certainly assisted us and Coach Morgan refused to adjust his game plan. He continued to call mostly pass plays despite the strong winds.

Three first-half turnovers—all inside the red zone—had helped us shut out one of the state's highest-scoring teams.

As we took the field in the second half, I couldn't help but think that after all those years of failing to win state, after six previous failures in the biggest game of the season, perhaps it was all part of God's plan to make *this* game, this *final game* at St. Mary's High School even more memorable, even sweeter than it would have otherwise been.

I believed we were a team of destiny. This was more than a game. This was something bigger. They might be able to take away our school, the job I loved, and my pension; but they wouldn't be able to take away a state title. They wouldn't be able to take away the fact that in their final game ever played, the St. Mary's Panthers finished as champions. Forever number one.

I said a quick Hail Mary, my way of asking God to make this dream a reality. A victory tonight would make an otherwise painful moment in Kingstown's history a bit more bearable. It would turn a tragic situation into a moment more special than it otherwise would have been. It would also be a lifelong lesson for these players and our entire community. It would be proof that good things can and do happen in the face of tragedy if you refuse to give up.

I'd spent thirty years teaching students that God would never allow something bad to happen if he couldn't bring a greater good out of it. In some mysterious way, perhaps *this* would be that greater good.

A championship tonight could have a positive effect on the entire community. A dose of pride like this could lead to any number of greater goods that I could not see.

Please, God, hear my prayer, I silently prayed. *Give*

these boys – and me – this moment. We need it. They deserve it.

I noticed that the snow had stopped and the wind had calmed down as the third quarter was set to begin. We just had to hold on. For twenty-four more minutes, we had to hold on.

39

We got the ball to start the third quarter and converted four third-down conversions to drive down to the 1-yard line. On a fourth-and-goal, we ran the option. Our quarterback gave it to the fullback who slammed forward and crossed the goal line. With five minutes left in the third quarter, we had a 21-0 lead.

Glendale Park didn't blink. They responded with a quick drive down the field and scored their first touchdown with two minutes to play in the third.

We got the ball back with a 21-7 lead and we drove to midfield before fumbling the ball on the last play of the third quarter. Glendale Park recovered the fumble and cut our lead to seven points just four plays later.

It was a gut-check moment for our team. It was now a one-score game in the fourth quarter and the momentum had shifted. We had to regain control.

Our option attack drove us back to midfield before we had to punt—a perfectly-executed punt which pinned the Trojans inside their own 10-yard line. They would be starting their drive at the 7-yard line with 6:41 left to play.

On the ensuing drive, we forced five third downs. Glendale Park converted on the first four; we stopped them on the fifth.

Faced with a fourth-and-six on our 15-yard line, the Trojans surprised no one by deciding to go for it. There was 2:03 left to play. This could be the game.

I could really use some wind right about now, I thought to myself. But the air was calm.

Glendale Park's quarterback took the shotgun snap, pump-faked a fade route to the end zone, and then rocketed the ball perfectly to his tight end who was cutting across the field. He caught it at the 10-yard line and then barreled over our defenders at the goal line.

Trailing 21-20, Coach Morgan shocked us all by leaving his offense on the field. He was going to try to take the lead here by scoring on a two-point conversion instead of risking overtime. It was a bold move, befitting of his personality.

We called timeout to make sure we had the right defensive alignment and personnel. I called over the head referee and said, "Keep an eye out for a pick play here; they love to run it in these situations." A "pick play" was an illegal version of a "rub route," where one offensive receiver purposely makes contact with a defender in order to free up another receiver. Run in this manner, it was considered offensive pass interference. It's a technically-illegal-but-often-used tactic—one that teams can frequently get away with because it's a judgment call by the official.

"Thanks for the advice," the referee said to me in a sarcastic tone that made it clear he didn't appreciate me trying to influence his call.

Sure enough, Glendale Park lined up and ran the exact same play I thought they would. Their outside receiver cut inside and slammed right into one of our defensive backs. The inside receiver cut to the outside and was wide open since his defender had been taken out of the play. Their quarterback rifled the ball in for the easy two-point score.

The Glendale Park fans erupted as the official raised his arms to signal that the Trojans had taken the lead, 22-21.

"Where's the flag?" I yelled to the referee.

"Where's the flag?!"

"Contact was incidental, Coach," he yelled back.

I was furious. It's one thing to miss a penalty, but quite another to miss it after being warned of the very penalty right before it happened.

"I want an explanation," I yelled, marching out onto the field.

"I gave you one," the referee yelled back sharply. "And if you take another step out here you're going to cost your team fifteen yards." He was threatening me with an unsportsmanlike conduct penalty.

I couldn't believe it. I was seeing red as my blood boiled.

Glendale Park had its first lead of the night, 22-21, with 1:53 left to play.

This can't be happening, I thought to myself. *Not again. Not another blown lead in the state championship. This CAN'T be happening.*

For a moment, I thought again that I might be cursed and that any other program looking to hire a head coach next season might be thinking the same thing about me.

I looked up to the sky — trying to calm down, but also praying for a miracle.

Before I could cool off from the blown call, Glendale Park had kicked the ball off. Our top running back was also our kick returner. He caught the ball at the 9-yard line. He made the first man miss. Then another. He picked up a huge block at the 25. Then, I saw a row of three blockers in front of him with only one defender between him and daylight.

The defender didn't have a chance. He was rolled over by our blockers and there was nothing but open field ahead for our return man. Just like that, we had regained the lead, 27-22.

Football, like life, can change in a heartbeat.

We really were a team of destiny.

We went for two after the touchdown and didn't convert, but we still had the lead. Now we needed to stop the vaunted Trojan offense.

This wasn't an easy task, as Glendale Park proved on its first play of the drive—a 26-yard completion that instantly put the Trojans back in our territory.

Two plays later, Glendale Park had the ball on our 32-yard-line with 1:15 left to play. They tried the same play they had scored a touchdown on earlier with the pump-fake deep before passing to their tight end crossing through the middle of the field. This time, we were ready.

Micky broke out of his zone and sprinted in front of the football to intercept it.

Our fans roared with cheers behind our sideline. We had just forced our fourth turnover of the night.

Could it be that Big Jim's own grandson would make the play that sealed this storied program's final victory? You couldn't draw it up any better than that.

All we had to do now was run out the clock.

With just over a minute left to play. We had a 27-22 lead and Glendale Park only had two timeouts left.

They used their first timeout after our first run, a 4-yard gain. They used their final timeout after our second-down run, a 3-yard gain.

It was third down-and-three-to-go with 0:52 left in the game. Glendale Park was out of timeouts. A first down here would seal the win for us.

We ran a triple option play and our quarterback read it beautifully. The dive back was taken and so was the pitch back. Our quarterback kept it himself and easily crossed the first-down line. He slid to the ground as one of the Glendale Park defenders dove at him.

Our fans let out a chorus of boos. There was a skirmish between players on the field after the play, but it wasn't clear to me what was going on.

"Throw the flag, that's a cheap shot," one of our coaches yelled, referring to the fact that the Glendale Park player hit our quarterback after he was already sliding to the ground.

The refs didn't respond. In fact, they were busy trying to unpile bodies following the post-play skirmish.

It took me a moment to realize what was going on.

A Trojan player was now jumping up and down with the football as his teammates celebrated. The officials were conferring in a huddle.

Finally, the referee emerged from the conference and signaled first down, Glendale Park.

Fans on both sides went nuts. Our side booing, their side cheering.

The officials ruled that our quarterback had fumbled the ball before he was down and that Glendale Park recovered the fumble.

My quarterback rushed over to the sidelines. "Coach, I was down!" he shouted. "I swear! I was down before he even hit me!"

He had tears in his eyes. He couldn't believe what was happening. None of us could.

Five plays later, with just four seconds left to play, Glendale Park's quarterback threw a fade route into the corner of the end zone. We had good coverage, but it was a perfect pass.

Glendale Park won the game, 28-27.

I met Coach Morgan at midfield for the obligatory post-game handshake. He was smiling big as he gripped my hand. "Keep your head up, Coach, you'll land somewhere."

His condescending tone made me want to slug him, but I pretended I didn't hear him and simply said, "Congratulations."

Jimmy, my oldest son and our team's running backs coach, had spent the game up in the coaches' box. As I was walking off the field, he met me and pulled me aside before I entered the locker room.

"They stole it from us, Dad, they stole it from us," Jimmy said. "They keep replaying it on TV. The announcers can't believe it. His knee was down on the ground and he had slid a full yard before he was hit and the ball popped loose. The refs took this one from us. They stole it from us. I can't believe it."

"I can," I said.

Before the game, I had told our players that they could take our school and they could take our team away from us, but they couldn't take away our effort, our attitude, and our pride. My point was that nobody could take away what we went out and *earned*.

Turns out, I was wrong. They *could* take away what we had earned.

40

In the locker room after the game, I told our players I was proud of them for giving it everything they had. I told them I didn't care what the scoreboard said; I knew they were champions on this night.

My words had little impact on the mood of the team. The players were devastated. As was I.

This all seemed so unfair. Just one hour before, we were up 21-0 in the state championship game and it all seemed so *meant to be*. Now, it felt like our school and our team was being kicked while we were down.

I went back into the coaches' office and shut the door. I needed a moment to regroup. This was all too much to take.

You just couldn't give us this, could you? I silently said to the heavens. *It's not enough that you're ripping our community apart, but you couldn't even give us the championship we earned? It's not enough to ruin our lives; you had to ruin our season, too, didn't you?*

I'm not sure if I was directing these questions at God or Big Jim. Probably both.

I thought you were going to help me tonight. This statement was directed at Big Jim. *Where were you when I needed you?*

For all the talk Big Jim preached about faith, family, hard work, and community; I had to wonder where those things were now.

Why didn't our community come together to save the school?

Why didn't our hard work pay off on the field tonight, as it should have?

If we're so strong when we work together as a family, why does everything we do seem to fail?

Perhaps everything Big Jim and I had preached through the years was nothing more than wishful thinking after all. Those things sounded great. It made you feel good to hear that everything would work out if we stuck together, worked hard, and kept our faith.

But when push came to shove, when the rubber met the road, it made little difference — on the football field or in life.

I wondered if everything I'd been through since Friday — seeing Big Jim in the church and then experiencing a completely different alternative life —

was nothing more than a vivid dream. It all felt so real at the time, but now the realness of it was fading and the results on the field told me Big Jim's promise to help was phony.

It was all just one crazy hallucination, my mind playing a trick on me, I thought to myself.

Perhaps it was my subconscious trying to convince myself that everything would turn out okay. *Delude* myself, is more like it.

After a few minutes of stewing in bitterness, there was a knock at the door.

"Come in," I said, rubbing my tired eyes.

Jimmy walked in and shut the door. He sat down in a chair across from the desk I was sitting behind.

"What is wrong with us?" he asked. "Are we cursed?"

"It sure feels like it, doesn't it?" I said.

After almost a minute of silence with both of us staring at the floor — still in disbelief as we replayed the game's final events in our heads — Jimmy asked, "Are you going to give *The Senior Speech*?"

I took a deep, exhausted breath before saying, "I told myself on the bus today that regardless of whether we won or lost tonight, I was going to give it. I told myself I had to do it. I told myself that now, more than ever, the boys needed to hear it despite—no, *because of*—everything that was going on. I came here believing that giving *The Senior Speech* would be the most important thing I did tonight..."

I paused.

"And now?" Jimmy asked.

"And now, I don't know...I don't know how I can go in there and tell them that as long as they follow their hearts, everything will end up alright. How can I? It obviously isn't true."

Jimmy didn't respond. His eyes were still focused on the floor. I couldn't tell whether he thought I should or shouldn't give the speech that had been given to every group of seniors to play for St. Mary's High School for the last six-plus decades.

"What would Big Jim do?" he finally asked.

I exhaled slowly. "We both know what he would do."

Jimmy nodded.

"But that doesn't mean it's the right thing to do," I said.

Jimmy snapped his head my way and looked at me like he didn't recognize me.

41

As our players showered up and gathered their equipment, I took questions at the post-game press conference. It took all the willpower I had to answer the media's questions as diplomatically as possible.

When asked about the fumble at the end of the game and whether I thought our quarterback was down, I said, "I haven't seen the replay. I'm sure the officials called the game to the best of their ability."

When asked about the rub route—or "pick play," as I preferred to call it—I said, "The official was right there, he said the contact was incidental and he has the final call."

When asked if I was happy with the officiating tonight, I simply said, "No comment."

When asked where I thought I'd be next season, I answered truthfully: "I have no idea."

When asked if losing this *seventh* state championship game felt worse than the other six, I responded with blunt honesty: "Yes."

When all the questions had been asked, I made

my way back to the locker room. Before opening the door, I took a deep breath.

"Okay, listen up," I said to the players who were now dressed and ready to board the busses that would take us back home for the final time. I looked over at Jimmy and saw his anxious face wondering what I was about to say.

"It's time to board the busses," I said. "Let's do this quickly."

Jimmy's shoulders dropped.

The players hesitantly began to shuffle towards the door.

In that moment, I saw Big Jim in my mind. We were back in the church pew. A tear running down his cheek. "I'm proud of you, son," he had said. "So proud."

And then I heard his voice almost as though he was standing right next to me, "Listen to your heart."

I knew what I had to do.

"Wait," I said to the team. "Seniors, stay behind. Underclassmen, wait for us on the bus."

When only the seniors remained in the locker room, I stepped in front of them and said, "Men, the reason I wait to give this speech until after the final game of the season is because I know you'll remember it for the rest of your lives…"

As some of the seniors cried and I choked back tears of my own, I gave the hardest *Senior Speech* I ever had to deliver.

42

The bus ride back to Kingstown was silent. It was as though we'd all just received our sentencing from the judge and the reality of it was settling in. I replayed the events of the game in my mind over and over again, knowing full well that I would be doing this for the next several months to come—as I always did after losing my final game of the season.

I also couldn't get Big Jim out of my head.

Where were you tonight? I wondered repeatedly. *Where was God? Why did things keep getting worse for us? What did I do to deserve this? Where were you tonight? Where are you NOW?*

As the bus rolled on, my bitterness turned back to worry. *What was I going to do next year? Where would I go from here? What would happen to my family and so many of the families I'd grown so close with over my lifetime?*

In my heart, I believed that giving *The Senior Speech* after the game was the right thing to do, but on this bus ride back to town I couldn't help but question again whether it was really the right advice to give these young men as they began the rest of their lives.

Is it SAFE to follow your heart? Do I truly believe that everything will work out for the best as long as we keep our priorities of faith, family, passion, health, and community straight? At the moment, it sure didn't feel like it. I wondered if everything I had just preached about faith, family, and following your heart was wishful thinking at best and nothing but a cruel lie at worst.

That's where trust comes in, I heard a voice inside say. *You have to trust. You have to have faith. You don't see the big picture. You don't see what's going on behind the scenes.*

I don't know where this voice came from—whether it was Big Jim or the Holy Spirit or simply a voice buried deep within my subconscious. All I know is that it was a voice of hope at a time when I needed to hear it badly.

You have to trust, the voice repeated. *You have to have faith.*

After two-and-a-half hours on the road, the bus took the Kingstown exit off the interstate. As we pulled into town, I noticed that one of the two lights that normally illuminated the WELCOME TO KINGSTOWN sign had burned out. How fitting this image was. The world was turning out the lights on Kingstown, Ohio.

We drove past the abandoned, weed-infested lot that was once home to Kingstown Steel and Pipe, the lifeblood of this town. It was gone and never coming back…just like I would soon be.

A deep sadness came over me as I realized just how much I was going to miss this place—even the ugly things about this town. For better or for worse, it was my hometown, the place I'd always belonged to.

You have to trust, I heard again. *You have to have faith.*

At that moment, I nodded and thought to myself, *What other choice do I have? I have to believe. I have to trust, just like Big Jim always told me to.*

Was I trying hard to convince myself that it was safe to have faith? Yes. But a funny thing happened. The more I told myself to believe it was safe to trust—that things would work out for the best—the more I *did* start to believe it.

The bus turned down Main Street and I noticed red flashing lights way up ahead. Stopped at a traffic light, I couldn't make out what was going on.

Was there an accident or a fire?

The bus lurched forward, slowed by traffic. It was odd to see this much traffic this late at night. It was nearly midnight in a town that didn't stay up late.

As we moved slowly towards the flashing lights, I realized that cars were parked at nearly every stall on Main Street. The red flashing lights were coming from several big red firetrucks and a few blue flashing lights were mixed in—those coming from police cars.

My heart skipped a beat—there had to have been an accident. From the looks of the commotion, it may have been a very bad one.

We were now just a few blocks away from all the flashing lights and I saw that dozens of cars were stopped up ahead. They weren't moving; they were parked right there in the middle of the street, blocking our normal path back to the school.

And I saw...*people*. A large crowd of people. People everywhere. There were hundreds of people gathered around the firetrucks.

As we got closer to the traffic jam of people and cars, I saw smiling faces and I heard honking horns. The large crowd of people noticed our bus and started clapping and cheering.

What in the world is going on? I thought to myself.

It looked like a victory parade was taking place.

"Do these people realize we *lost* the game?" I heard Jimmy ask.

The players on the bus were standing now, everyone wondering what this enthusiastic crowd had gathered for.

When the bus could no longer move forward due to the wave of people who were heading our way, it came to a complete stop, about a block before our scheduled turn on 2nd Street.

The crowd cheered with delight. I saw fists pumping in the air and the crowd then broke into a chant: "Go big blue! Go big blue!"

"I guess this is the end of the road," our bus driver said.

I got up, walked to the door, and he opened it with his lever.

The crowd roared as the door opened and I stepped down from the bus.

"We did it, Coach, we did it!" I heard someone say.

"Can you believe this?" another fan shouted my way.

"What is going on?" I asked nobody in particular.

I felt pats on my back as the crowd parted to make way for me and the team.

"And there they are, your St. Mary's Panthers!" This was an amplified voice, like someone using a megaphone up ahead. It was a familiar voice. It was…Alonzo's voice.

I could now see Alonzo up ahead, standing in the bed of somebody's pickup truck parked next to one of the firetrucks. He was speaking into a CB-like microphone that was attached to the firetruck's cab. He was waving us towards him.

"Let's all make room for Coach Callahan and the boys in blue," his amplified voice said to the crowd.

As I got closer, Alonzo was laughing so hard he had to lean over. Apparently, the confused look on my face was just too much for him.

When I got to the pickup truck, I saw Gina standing beside it. She had tears in her eyes — tears of joy. She hugged me hard and whispered, "We did it!"

I asked her, "Did what?"

Before she could answer, Alonzo had already grabbed my hand and a few fans behind me helped boost me up to join Alonzo on the truck bed.

I leaned in close to Alonzo and said, "You mind telling me what the hell is going on?"

He responded with a laugh and I smiled for the first time in hours, still not sure what everyone was so happy about.

"Coach," he said to my ear, "you gotta' start checking your phone after games."

On game days, I always turned my phone off hours prior to kickoff and I made it a habit to not turn it back on until the following morning. Win or lose, I needed time to rebalance my emotions before answering calls and messages. We had a strict no-cellphone policy for the coaches and players as well on game day. For the past six hours, our entire team had been cut off from the outside world.

Now standing on the truck bed next to Alonzo, the crowd cheered as I hesitantly waved. I was still confused about what everyone was so happy about.

"Did the state reverse the game's outcome?" I

asked Alonzo.

"No," he said. "Something much better."

He laughed again. *What was I missing?*

"Coach wants to know what's going on," Alonzo said into the mic.

The crowd cheered with laughter.

"Why don't we let someone else clue him in," Alonzo said, his voice echoing down Main Street. "Is there another Callahan who would like to say a few words?"

I turned around to see my brother, Andy, walking up beside me. In all the commotion and confusion, I hadn't noticed him standing near the truck.

He hopped up to join Alonzo and me.

"Andy," I said as I hugged my brother tight. "What are you doing here? Did you get my message last night?"

Andy nodded with a smile and said, "I did, and I'm sorry too."

Before he could say another word, Alonzo gave Andy the mic.

"My big brother wants to know what I'm doing here," Andy said — to me and the crowd.

"And I suppose many of you would like an

explanation about exactly what has happened over the past twenty-four hours," Andy continued as the crowd gave its approval.

"On Thursday night, I had a dream," he said, the crowd quieting now. "I know it sounds crazy, but in my dream I talked to my father, Big Jim Callahan."

My eyes widened, I couldn't believe what I was hearing.

"Now, if I tell you all too much about this dream, everybody's going to think I'm crazy," Andy said. "But let me just say that Big Jim showed me—for the first time in a long time—that I'd forgotten about the things that are most important in life. Any of you that played for my dad or my brother know what I'm talking about."

Men throughout the crowd nodded, acknowledging the famous *Senior Speech* and the constant reminders that faith, family, courage, and character were the most important values in one's life.

Andy continued, "I had no idea about the horrible news that St. Mary's was closing until…until Big Jim told me in my dream."

Several in the crowd gasped.

"It's true." Andy nodded. "I know it sounds crazy, but it's true.

"When I woke up, I checked the Internet and, sure enough, I saw it was really happening. When I saw this, I was flooded by warm memories of all the people in this community who helped me growing up. I remembered all the good people who took time out of their day to encourage me. I remembered my classmates, my teachers, my coaches, and even perfect strangers who genuinely *cared* about me.

"I have to tell you, I've traveled all over the world and I've spent time in just about every major city in this country. From everything I've seen, I can tell you that what you have here in Kingstown is rare. *Extremely* rare. People don't know how special this place is. They don't know about the sacrifices people make for each other in a town like this. And they don't know how important St. Mary's High School is to this community."

The crowd cheered and I heard a few random "go big blue" chants.

Andy smiled and motioned for the crowd to quiet down. "When we talk about the importance of faith and family in this town, we mean what we say.

We're all a part of the St. Mary's family. And when one of our brothers or sisters falls down, we come together to help them up!"

I heard more applause and saw more tears in the eyes of the crowd.

"I'm ashamed to admit that until a couple nights ago, I had completely lost track of these values," Andy said. "I spent the last twenty-five years of my life running from this place, thinking that I'd find happiness and success by cutting my ties to this place. But the truth is, I've never stopped thinking about Kingstown and St. Mary's. Something about this place, this community, this *family*; it keeps calling me back.

"When I heard what was going on with St. Mary's, I felt like it was, in some way, my fault. *I* was one of the reasons it was closing. *I*, like too many others who have left this place and never come back, had abandoned the community that raised me. I knew I had to do something.

"I called a friend at the *Wall Street Journal* who owed me a favor. I told him what was going on, I told him what a tragedy it was, and I asked him to help me get the word out pronto. He went to work and published a story about our town and our school. Many of you saw that wonderful article this morning."

Most in the crowd applauded this fact; I was still clueless about the article.

"From there, ESPN picked up the story," Andy continued. "Next thing you know, the story of this school went viral. We even became a hashtag on Twitter: #SaveStMarys."

Some in the crowd cheered, some laughed, and some clearly had no idea what a hashtag was.

"What happened after that is nothing short of a miracle." Andy paused to gather himself, becoming overwhelmed with emotion. "I just want you all to know what a tremendous impact you've had on me.

"And John," Andy turned to me, still speaking into the mic. "You've had a tremendous impact on me as well. When I see you and how you're living your life, I see a man who is doing things the right way. In so many ways that I've never told you before, I've always looked up to you—*always*. And I couldn't bear to let you go through this alone."

I hugged my brother, not stopping to think how odd it might seem to share an emotional reunion like this in front of several hundred people.

Alonzo grabbed the mic. "I still don't think Coach realizes what is going on."

"Maybe I can help," said another voice from the crowd. I looked down to see Ricky Walsh pulling himself up to our makeshift stage in the bed of this pickup truck.

When the crowd saw Ricky, I heard some grumbles and a few more gasps, but mostly shocked silence.

Ricky grabbed the mic with the aura of confidence he always had.

"I know I'm not the most popular guy to ever grow up in this town," Ricky said to the mic. "I know I've treated a lot of your horribly wrong. I was immature and arrogant and I said some horrible things about this place.

"Truthfully, I miss this place. I really do. I realize now how lucky I was to grow up here, to walk the halls of St. Mary's High, and to be coached by John Callahan. The lessons I learned here from Coach, from St. Mary's, and from all of you growing up—I didn't want to listen at the time. I didn't think I needed help from anybody. I wanted to go my own way.

"What I realize now is that by not listening to those lessons, but doing only what I thought would benefit me...well...it all led me down a very destructive path. It almost cost me my life."

The crowd was completely silent.

"I've been thinking about coming back here for a while now," Ricky continued. "I was wondering how I would do it. How could I ask all of you to forgive me? How could I ask all of you to accept me back after the way I behaved and the things that I said?

"When I saw the story on ESPN, when I saw Save St. Mary's trending online, and when I saw the GoFundMe page everybody was talking about, I knew what I had to do."

I now understood what was going on. Andy had started it and the ripple effect Big Jim always talked about took our story nationwide overnight.

"I stand here today asking for your forgiveness," Ricky said. "I'm sorry for the things I've said and any hurt that I've caused you. I'm trying hard to turn my life around, but I need a community. I need *this* community to help me. And I promise to do my part too."

The people in the streets applauded in response to Ricky's apology.

"We're here for you, Ricky," I said, patting him on the back.

"Thank you, Coach," he said with watery eyes. "And thank you for all that you taught me.

"Oh yeah, and one more thing," Ricky said—now into the mic. "The rumors aren't true about me blowing through all my money."

With that, he reached into his pocket and handed Alonzo a check. He then climbed down from the truck and made his way into the crowd receiving pats, handshakes, and hugs along the way.

Alonzo unfolded the check. His eyes bulged and he stumbled backward, acting as though he might faint before smiling big.

Alonzo took the mic again. "Ricky Walsh has just donated five...I almost can't say it...five *million* dollars to our cause."

The crowd erupted with cheers!

"That brings us to..." Alonzo checked his phone to get the latest figure. "That brings us to seventeen *million* and counting!"

Cheers poured over Main Street.

I couldn't believe what I was hearing. How could this happen? How could this little school in this Rust Belt town raise so much money?

"This school is saved!" Alonzo yelled into the mic to more cheers and impromptu dancing in the streets. "This *family* is saved!"

43

"How about a few words from Coach Callahan?" Alonzo said into the microphone.

The crowd clapped and I took the mic.

"I don't know where to begin," I said. "I'm still trying to process what has happened. I'm...I'm overwhelmed."

I took a moment to gather myself and choke back tears of joy. "When I was told that St. Mary's High School would be shut down, it felt like a part of me—a part of who I was—was being ripped away from me. I know you all felt the same way."

I noticed people in the crowd who had played for me and for Big Jim. Some of the people I saw were *older* than Big Jim. Their sons, daughters, grandsons, and granddaughters went to St. Mary's and they wanted their great-grandchildren to go there as well.

"My whole life has been about St. Mary's High," I continued. "And, as I've told everyone—players, students, parishioners, fans, and anybody else who would listen—St. Mary's is a *family*. It's a family that can't be torn apart.

"And all my life I believed that.

"Until a couple nights ago.

"The news that St. Mary's would be shut down made me question everything about my life. It made me question the very things I'd been telling people for as long as I've been here. It made me question everything my dad, Big Jim, had taught me and so many of you. Tonight's state championship game only made the pain of those questions worse.

"It all made me question whether it was wise to follow your heart. To be perfectly honest, it made me wonder whether it was really *safe* to trust God."

The crowd was silent and I saw tears running down Gina's cheeks.

"I suppose it was that dark night of the soul that so many of us go through," I said. "And you know what? I didn't pass the test. I allowed my faith to waver. I lost my courage. I lost my faith.

"But tonight, you all are reminding me what faith really is. Tonight, I'm seeing what family is."

Many in the crowd applauded.

"They say when you ask God for a miracle, his preferred method of delivering that miracle is through the hands of other people, our neighbors. How often we lose sight of that. We think we all have to do it on our own. Or, we want God to come down and instantly fix everything. We don't want to have to rely on our neighbors. We don't want to have to ask others for help. We don't want to have to ask ourselves, 'What can *I* do for my neighbor.' We fall into self-pity and hopelessness.

"But the fact is, God goes to work when we go to work for each other. Miracles occur when we sacrifice for one another. Good things happen when we admit our vulnerabilities and we ask each other for help.

"Only when we follow what's true in our hearts and come together, like a *family*, will we ever find true success.

"You all have taught me today that this family can never be torn apart. This family is too strong. This family is there for one another when one of us gets knocked down!

"Together, there is nothing that this family can't accomplish!"

The crowd cheered, hugged, and high-fived each other.

"Thank you all so, so much for your sacrifices and your help."

I backed away from the mic just before letting my tears of joy fall freely.

Despite the frigid temperatures, the entire community celebrated late into the night.

That night, I saw Charlie Kowalski rip up the FOR SALE sign he had placed on the front window of Bob's Diner just a couple nights ago.

I learned that Mike Murphy, the owner of Victory Sportswear, had gone into his life savings to donate more than $100,000 before the national fundraising effort had gone viral. He made the donation on nothing but faith, knowing that it would only make a small dent in the amount needed to be raised.

I learned that as soon as Andy heard what was going on, he made it his mission to raise the money needed. He reached out to all his wealthy clients and put in $1 million of his own money to launch the GoFundMe page. Andy knew how to raise money and he put his skills to work in order to save the school, the community, and our jobs.

The story Andy had urged his friend at the *Wall Street Journal* to write was a nostalgic piece about the way things used to be in places like Kingstown, Ohio, and at schools like St. Mary's. It made the argument that things could *still* be that way if people made places like that a priority. It then mentioned the GoFundMe page and talked about the employees and former employees who would all lose their retirements if the school didn't raise money now. It quoted Andy, who said, "They don't make places like St. Mary's High anymore. If you still value things like faith, family, and community, I urge you to contribute to saving this school. Every little bit helps."

The article ended with a clever line about how some of Wall Street's wealthiest were already making sizable contributions. As Andy later told me, nothing gets a wealthy guy to give money faster than letting him know that other wealthy guys are already giving some. "They all want to out-do each other," Andy said.

Once the article went live, people all over the country started donating. Former players and alumni who lived elsewhere heard what was going on and offered what they could. Donations of $50, $100, $1,000, and even an occasional $10,000 added up quickly.

Complete strangers heard the story about this town, this community, and this school. *Sports Illustrated* and ESPN ran particularly touching online reports of the impact this school had on people during the Industrial Midwest's decline. Strangers saw this and felt compelled to make donations.

Andy's clients made particularly large donations.

I was later told that the $9.8 million figure was hit shortly after our state championship game had ended — a time when I would have been sitting in the coach's office after the game, asking myself why Big Jim hadn't helped me and stewing about why our community hadn't come together to save our beloved school. If only I had known what was really going on at that moment.

As soon as Alonzo saw that the financial goal was reached, he got on the phone with the archdiocese and got confirmation that the school would indeed be able to stay open.

Over the next several weeks, the donations continued to pour in from across the country. Major media outlets showed up to tell our story and with each mention online or on TV, more donations followed.

Ricky Walsh, in particular, became the feel-good sports story of the holiday season. He was turning his life around and trying to reach kids with his story about the dangers of drug use. The sports networks all did features on Ricky during their football pregame shows.

By the time the New Year arrived, more than $20 million had been put into a trust for St. Mary's High School. It was enough to save the school, save our pensions, and stabilize the school's budget for years to come.

Over the next several months, I noticed that all the good press about the Midwestern values of faith, family, and community keeping this town and this school alive led to more people moving back to Kingstown. On my evening walks, I'd run into former students and players that I hadn't seen in years. They'd tell me they decided to come back after being reminded what made this community so special.

One night, a complete stranger with his wife and kids stopped me on one of my walks down Main Street and told me they were thinking about moving to our small town after seeing the stories about us. He asked me what I thought. I smiled and told him he should follow his heart.

And just a few weeks ago, Andy called me from Florida to tell me he was selling his business and retiring from the financial game.

He told me that when he came back that weekend of the state championship he rekindled an old high school crush of his. They stayed in contact over the months that followed and he was thinking of moving back to Kingstown.

"That would be great," I said. "And you know, the school could use a good finance officer."

He laughed and said, "And I hear Patti is looking to book a regular band at her pub. Who says you can't find work in Kingstown?"

Every once in a while, I have nightmares that I'm living the alternative life Big Jim showed me. Whenever that happens, I wake up in a panic. Then, I look over and see my sweet Gina breathing softly next to me. I exhale a sigh of relief and hug her tight, thankful that I am where I am.

Thankful that I listened to my heart and that I

never lost track of my priorities.

As Big Jim had promised, when you follow your heart, keep your priorities straight, and live *your* unique purpose, good things happen.

You just have to trust.

About the Author

DARRIN DONNELLY is a writer and entrepreneur. He and his products have been featured in publications such as *The Wall Street Journal*, *Sports Illustrated*, *Fast Company Magazine*, and newspapers, websites, and radio outlets all over the world. He lives in Kansas City with his wife and three children.

Donnelly can be reached at *SportsForTheSoul.com* or on Twitter: @DarrinDonnelly.

Sports for the Soul

Stories of Faith, Family, Courage, and Character.

This book is part of the *Sports for the Soul* series. For updates on this book, a sneak peek at future books, and a free newsletter that delivers advice and inspiration from top coaches, athletes, and sports psychologists, join us at: **SportsForTheSoul.com**.

The *Sports for the Soul* newsletter will help you:

- Find your calling and follow your passion

- Harness the power of positive thinking

- Build your self-confidence

- Attack every day with joy and enthusiasm

- Develop mental toughness

- Increase your energy and stay motivated

- Explore the spiritual side of success

- Be a positive leader for your family and your team

- Become the best version of yourself

- And much more…

Join us at: **SportsForTheSoul.com**.

Think Like a Warrior

by Darrin Donnelly

In this bestselling inspirational fable, Chris McNeely is a college football coach who is at the end of his rope after a hard-and-fast fall from the top of his profession. Now bankrupt and on the verge of losing his job, he has no idea what he's doing wrong or how to get back on track.

Angry, worried, and desperate for help, McNeely receives mysterious visits from five of history's greatest coaches: **John Wooden, Buck O'Neil, Herb Brooks, Bear Bryant, and Vince Lombardi.** Together, these five legendary leaders teach McNeely how to take control of his life with the five inner beliefs shared by the world's most successful people.

The "warrior mindset" he develops changes his life forever— and it will change yours as well.

Book No. 2 in the *Sports for the Soul* series…

Old School Grit
by Darrin Donnelly

Bob Flanagan, a legendary college basketball coach who thinks like John Wooden and talks like Mike Ditka, represents the voice of OLD SCHOOL GRIT. While his team tries to advance through the NCAA postseason tournament, Flanagan uses his last days as a coach to write his grandchildren letters revealing the rules for a successful and happy life. The rules of grit.

Flanagan lives by the old school code of faith, family, courage, and character. He believes people give up too easily these days and his letters are a rallying cry for toughening up and building grit. The 15 rules revealed in this book provide a clear path to success in any endeavor.

Consider this book an instruction manual for getting back to the values that truly lead to success and developing the type of old school grit that will get you through anything.

Book No. 3 in the *Sports for the Soul* series…

Relentless Optimism
by Darrin Donnelly

In this bestselling book, you'll meet Bobby Kane, a minor league baseball player who realizes his dream of making it to the majors is finally coming to a disappointing end. That is, until he meets an unconventional manager named Wally Hogan. More mental coach than baseball manager, Wally teaches Bobby that if you want to change your life, you have to first change your thinking.

Wally shows Bobby what it takes to maintain a positive attitude through the ups and downs of life. He teaches him proven, real-world techniques for building and sustaining optimism throughout life's peaks and valleys. These methods have an immediate impact on Bobby's life and they will have an immediate impact on yours as well.

This book will teach you how to use positive thinking to make your dreams come true.

Made in the USA
Columbia, SC
17 January 2020